THE ART OF THE MINIATURE

THE ART OF THE
MINIATURE

Small Worlds and How to Make Them

JANE FREEMAN

Foreword by ROGER ROSENBLATT

WATSON-GUPTILL PUBLICATIONS / NEW YORK

To the memory of my parents, Ann and Joe, and to my family: Linda, Elizabeth, Kathryn, Arthur, Andy, Walter, and Joseph Matthew, with love;

    to Swami Chidvilasananda, with gratitude for her endless fount of wisdom, love, and inspiration;

    and to the memory of the World Trade Center, which stood in my backyard as a daily source of inspiration and upliftment, and to everyone who perished on September 11, 2001.

Senior Editor: Joy Aquilino
Project Editor: Anne McNamara
Designer: Barbara Balch
Graphic production: Hector Campbell
Text set in 11/14.5 Adobe Garamond

First published in 2002 by Watson-Guptill Publications,
a division of VNU Business Media, Inc.,
770 Broadway, New York, N.Y. 10003
www.watsonguptill.com

THE FOREWORD by Roger Rosenblatt (pages 8–9) is adapted from a television essay on the work of Jane Freeman that originally aired on November 1, 1999, on *The NewsHour with Jim Lehrer.* Courtesy of MacNeil/Lehrer Productions and Roger Rosenblatt.

Some of the information in Part III (pages 76–122) was adapted from "Workshop Wisdom" tips that were originally published in *Dollhouse Miniatures* magazine, a division of Kalmbach Publishing Company, and is used with express permission.

Library of Congress Cataloging-in-Publication Data
Freeman, Jane.
    The art of the miniature : small worlds and how to make them / Jane
Freeman ; foreword by Roger Rosenblatt.
       p. cm.
Includes bibliographical references and index.
   ISBN 0-8230-0309-4
1. Miniature craft. 2. Miniature rooms. I. Title
   TT178. F74 2002
   745.5928—dc21

                           2001006304

Manufactured in Malaysia

First printing, 2002

1 2 3 4 5 6 7 8 9 / 10 09 08 07 06 05 04 03 02

Notes on the Illustrations
All of the works illustrated are copyrighted by the individual artists or institutions unless otherwise stated.

All uncredited works copyright © by Jane Freeman. The illustrations of Jane Freeman's works on pages 2, 3, 9, 19–23, 32, 37, 39, 42, 43 (top), 47, 49, 54, 59, 60 66, 67 (top), 73, 74–75, 76, 77, 81, 84, 89, 90 (bottom), 91, 95, 97, 108, 112 (bottom), 115–117, 119 (top), and 121 were originally published in *Dollhouse Miniatures* magazine, a division of Kalmbach Publishing Company, and are used with express permission.

Page 1: SUBWAY, 1993. 2¾ x 4¼ x 1 inches. Private collection. *A shower door pull made into a train station.*
Page 2: Detail, LECHEROUS APPETITES: THE BANQUET SCENE, 2000. 18½ x 25½ x 18 inches (entire structure). *Inspired by Mozart's opera* Don Giovanni. *See page 49 for the entire piece.*
Page 3: SARASTRO'S SUN (FINALE) from THE MAGIC FLUTE series, 1997–99. 20 x 20 x 14 inches.

ACKNOWLEDGMENTS

This project initially was to include only my work. I was visiting art galleries as I wrote this book, and discovered others working in miniature, whom I felt should be included. Their work supports and expands my premise that the miniature is a fine art as much as painting and sculpture. Thanks to the artists who contributed to this book: Rosemary Butler, Eric Edelman, Katharine Forsyth, Susan Leopold, David Levinthal, Victoria and Richard MacKenzie-Childs, John Mackiewicz, Barbara Minch, Charles Mingus III, Diane Price, Tim Prythero, David Malcolm Rose, and Alan Wolfson.

Thanks to Kristen Scheuing, Deborah Hufford, and Sybil Harp of Kalmbach Publishing for their support at *Dollhouse Miniatures* magazine. Thanks to Gail Levin and John Van Sickle for photographing the miniature *Fireplace Garden* for this book. I'm grateful to Eric Edelman and Abigayl Sperber for editorial suggestions, for providing the section on lighting, and for obtaining the rights for us to use the Joseph Cornell image in this book. Permission also came from VAGA, Inc.; Yuki Puar of C&M Arts, who loaned the photograph; and Donald Windham, the owner of the Cornell.

Thanks to Joan Ann Mrazik for the miniature food she's made for my art. Thanks to Ichiro Kurihara for his translation of Basho's haiku, for his help in understanding the concept of *shibui,* and for providing the documentary on miniature-making in Japan. Gordon Gilbert made

the diagrams that appear on page 104, for which I am grateful. Thanks for the friendship of Renée McKenna and Katharine Forsyth at Dollhouse Antics.

Even before this project began I enjoyed the support of my writing group upstate—Peggy Bendet, Lori Shivali Tomsic, Angela Zusman, Nada Clyne, Megan Radha Bird, and Rudra Sharp. I also appreciate the editorial suggestions of Anthony Bond, who read the manuscript with the sensitivity and precision of a fine writer.

Thanks to my photographers, whose work appears throughout this book: Brit Bunkley, Peter Jacobs, John Berens, and Sean Hemmerle from the James Dee Studio. Thanks to the woodworkers who built many of the stages, boxes and shells: Steve White (artist, inventor, and friend), Stefan Petrik, and David Dunn.

Thanks to the people who worked on this book: Anne McNamara, whose sharp eye and gift for organization helped the manuscript; Barbara Balch, whose elegant design beautifully complements the text and images; and of course Joy Aquilino, my talented and serene editor at Watson-Guptill, with whom I shared many a giggle during the writing of this book.

Thanks to the late Laurence Donovan, artist, poet, mentor, and friend.

SHRINE, 1991. 5½ x 4½ x 3¼ inches. Private collection. *The box is a wooden saki cup. The roof is a heavy brass hardware plate, with two brass drawer pulls and electrical gizmos.*

CONTENTS

CAROUSEL TICKETS, 1995.
12 x 8 x 6 inches.

PART III

PASS THE GLUE:
THINGS TO MAKE, AND MAKING THINGS 74

BAZZINI's (front and back),
1993. 17 x 13 x 12 inches.
Private collection. *Portrait of
a building on Greenwich Street
in New York.*

FOREWORD

"UNOCCUPIED ROOMS" BY ROGER ROSENBLATT

Jane Freeman is an artist of small worlds who since the mid-1980s has been creating a way to understand one's place in one's life. Freeman creates miniature rooms that contain everything but people. Yet they are not dollhouses minus the dolls. Rather, they are undersized structures that demand oversize imaginations. We are the people inside them. And at the same time, we are outside, too. We are in and out of the vacant lot in *Night Prowl;* in and out of her homage to Matisse's *Red Studio;* players and audience in her scenes from *The Magic Flute;* lingerers and observers in Van Gogh's *Bedroom in Arles.* We live and do not live in the *Lower East Side Tenement;* ride and do not ride the subway in *Below the City.*

In all her created universe, she creates a proposition: People are outside the world they live in. This paradox seems modernist, but it goes back and forward forever. There is a great deal more than cleverness in her work, but her work is exceptionally clever. She sees small, and has a near-magical ability to discover in the larger world objects that become other things in hers: tea bags, napkin rings, toys, scraps of wire and wood, nails. In her small studio, which she does occupy in New York City's Tribeca, I asked her to detail what went into her *Subway Platform.* "The girders are made out of shelf brackets. Heater filter backs are the fences. Bic lighters for the subway turnstiles. Orthodontia molds for the

subway tunnels. There's a Swatch watch up here that's the clock. There's a sink aerator here, which is perfect for the PA system—looks just like it."

That eye of hers allows her to make visual jokes—puns—in her work. But more important is the cosmic joke she deals with: that we never really know where we are, even when we are responsible for where we are. In any room one occupies, one is aware of part of the room, but never the whole. The room is one's life. The room is the graveyard in *Don Giovanni,* or a television studio, or Rousseau's *Dream.* Or it is the room you are in right now. You know something of what it says about you—the biography is implied. But it is also incomplete. You don't know where you fit in, exactly. You are not sure of your place in the world, in spite of the fact that you have made or chosen that place. In a sense, then, one creates all the evidence of a life, except oneself. One goes on a lifelong hunt to find small, substantial things, like one's soul.

Commenting on the spiritual element in her work, Freeman said, "It's like if you go into a vast, beautiful cathedral, you become overwhelmed, because it's like experiencing the dazzlement of the whole cosmos. So you find something small—an altar, a sculpture, a statue, a candle—to center yourself on. And in doing so, without losing any of the awe, but all of the overwhelmed feeling, you

find yourself. And you discover that you aren't so small after all."

What Freeman does with this special form of art is to make one suddenly aware of the place of place in a life, of the effort to locate one's self on a number of levels, and we try to learn how to live. We all begin as unoccupied rooms. Freeman is openly driven by the fact that she finds the world beautiful, even when the world's rooms are spare, cold, or menacing, and she discloses a beauty in every scrap she uses. Yet the unfathomable, imponderable beauty of the world lies in the people she does not create, who struggle to know where they are. Like Freeman, they too construct rooms out of everything they come upon, and then yearn to enter the lives they make.

Roger Rosenblatt began writing professionally in his mid-thirties, when he became Literary Editor and a columnist for *The New Republic*. Before that, he taught at Harvard, where he earned his Ph.D. and was Briggs-Copeland Professor of English. Since 1980, his essays for *Time* magazine have won two George Polk Awards, awards from the Overseas Press Club, the American Bar Association, and many others. His television essays for the *NewsHour with Jim Lehrer* on PBS have won the George Foster Peabody Award and the Emmy. He is the author of seven books, including the national bestseller *Rules for Aging*. The *Chicago Tribune* has called his essays and stories "magazine journalism as an art form," and William Safire of the *New York Times* wrote that his work represents "some of the most profound and stylish writing in America today."

TRIAL BY FIRE AND WATER (CATACOMB UNDER CENTRAL PARK) from THE MAGIC FLUTE series, 1997–99. 26 x 27 x 18 inches. *Each side is separately lit, and each gate opens independently to feature the two trials sequentially. The knights are copied from the drawing for the original production.*

PREFACE

This book is for anyone interested in experimenting with the possibilities inherent in working in miniature scale. To adapt Alexander Calder's words about his mobiles, making miniatures is like engaging in "a little private celebration." And anybody can join the celebration— all that's required is the desire to do so. If you've ever put together a scrapbook, reorganized a closet, planned a garden, or rearranged your living room, you can create a miniature interior or landscape. Even if you've never drawn a picture, you already may be a burgeoning miniaturist, with an accumulation of fancy cocktail picks, matchboxes, gold charms—or postage stamps so beautiful you've wished you could frame them. Well, you *can* frame them, and even build a marvelous setting for them—a bedroom, city park, crystal grotto, or any place you please. And, if you're the frugal type, you'll delight in inventing rare, rich-looking tableaux out of common paraphernalia, converting what the French call *objets trouvés* into *objets d'art!*

By miniature scale, I generally mean one inch equals a foot, which has long been standard dollhouse scale. But one-inch scale need not be rigidly adhered to. Other scales, and mixtures of scales, are represented in this book.

The varied points of view offered by the other artists in this book represent a few of the countless stylistic approaches to creating in miniature: Alan Wolfson is a photorealist whose uncanny urban scenes brilliantly exploit techniques like forced perspective and multiple views. Barbara Minch's shrine-like palaces incorporate painting and photography. Rosemary Butler makes Dada-esque assemblages layered with symbolism. John Mackiewicz's gritty city vignettes are enhanced by ingenious lighting tricks and manipulations of paint. Tim Prythero creates complex urban scenes of astonishing realism, and David Malcolm Rose records the defunct roadside services he's photographed along America's "Lost Highways." Charles Mingus III and Eric Edelman work in ways that suggest a Surrealist influence. David Levinthal's nocturnal, mysterious tableaux are akin to *film noir*. Katharine Forsyth offers a humorous example of "distressing" new dollhouse furniture to make it look old. Susan Leopold constructs unsettling private and public spaces, while Diane Price creates rustic, intimate interiors. The masterpiece rooms built by Victoria and Richard MacKenzie-Childs are capricious, opulent, and lushly fantastical. And my own work leans toward painterly expressionism.

It's clear that the genre of miniature art is as individually expressive as all traditional mediums of fine art, and that working in small scale, one can transcend the limits of the factual architectural

model, or the mimetic toy or display dollhouse. Models that merely exploit technical virtuosity or pristine fact can be predictable, tedious, or psychologically airless. The Thorne collection of miniature rooms at the Art Institute of Chicago are indeed exquisite; technically they exemplify the zenith of artisanship, interior decoration, and design authenticity. But as Matisse said, "Exactitude is not truth." And truth is what the artist invariably seeks.

Art has a different intention than the functional. It is first and foremost a vehicle of individual expression. Instead of creating factual reconstructions, my miniatures aim toward capturing the redolence of a place, real or imaginary, whether palace or slum.

Even so, true greatness is truly great, in any medium or for any purpose. The miniaturist ought to look at great architectural models, like the gorgeous wooden cathedral maquettes from the Italian Renaissance, or antique miniature Shinto shrines. These works can be a rich source of ideas, inspiration, and information, and certainly will be of interest to anyone creating in miniature.

Whether you're a working artist or becoming one, the intention of this book is to reawaken creativity through the genre of the miniature construction. Its aim is to activate the inventiveness of your vision. Creativity is everyone's birthright, as is proved by the unfailing astonishment of children's art. Too often as adults we forget our natural gifts and, before we know it, they are locked inside us like treasures in a safe. I hope this book will help you find the combination to your safe, so that you might reclaim the largesse of your own creative expression.

INTRODUCTION

FROM THE INFINITE TO THE INFINITESIMAL

EGYPTIAN. MODEL OF HOUSE
AND GARDEN. From the Tomb
of Mekutra (Meket-Re),
Thebes. Dynasty II, ca.
2009–1998 B.C. Wood,
painted and gessoed. Pool:
copper lined. Height 15½
inches (39.5 cm.). The
Metropolitan Museum of Art,
Rogers Fund and Edward S.
Harkness Gift, 1920. (20.3.13)
Photograph © 1992 The
Metropolitan Museum of Art.

One of the smallest microcosms I can think of is William Blake's "world in a grain of sand." It's a supreme concept, and reminds me of sculptures I once saw in a museum—breathtaking, realistic figures the size of grains of rice, in thimble-tiny settings that had to be viewed through a magnifying glass. I was impressed with the art, but I was equally impressed with the throngs patiently waiting to glimpse such stunning morsels. I was reminded that miniatures are and always have been cherished. Everywhere I turn, I find examples of and references to small worlds: snow globes and music boxes, altars and crèches, aquariums and terrariums, scale-model vehicles, key-chain baubles, birdhouses, souvenir monuments, toy theaters, refrigerator magnets. Why do miniatures possess such allure and trigger such a passionate response?

Maybe it's because seeing small is a way for us to order the world and to understand our place in the cosmos. Relating to tiny worlds elicits all sorts of uplifting and stimulating perspectives, emotions, and moods—thrill, poignancy, solace, perplexity, humor, wonder. In his commentary on the Queen Mary's Dolls' House in Windsor Castle, one of the most famous miniatures in the world, Clifford Musgrave wrote: "There is an extraordinary fascination and charm about smallness . . . a special satisfaction in creating a tiny replica of any object."

Art in miniature survives from ancient Egypt in an endearing house and garden, about 4,000 years old, in the collection of the Metropolitan Museum of Art. Miniatures like this were often buried with the dead for use in the afterlife. Tiny pieces of bronze furniture from ancient Greece and Rome have also been found. Some historians believe that dollhouses originated in Italy, because of their similarity to Early Christian crèches.

One of the earliest dollhouses on record was commissioned in 1558 by a Bavarian duke. It was originally intended for his daughter, but upon seeing this masterpiece, the duke decided to keep it for his art chamber. By then, a trend for miniaturization had begun, signaled by the printing of tiny books. Diane Purkiss writes in *Troublesome Things*: "Such productions offered to encapsulate the whole

world in a small portable artifact through the principle that the microcosm reflected the macrocosm." In 17th-century Holland, collecting small treasures became a fad among the wealthy. These objects were housed in specially built cabinets with partitions added to make decorated rooms.

Of countless allusions to miniatures in the visual arts, one outstanding example is *The Arnolfini Wedding* by Jan Van Eyck, an intriguing 15th-century painting in The National Gallery, London. A wedding is taking place in a lavish bedchamber, which is reflected, in its miniature entirety, in a convex mirror. This seemingly incidental background object is crucial to the meaning of the painting, for it reveals more than what appears in the picture plane: we can see two otherwise invisible witnesses standing outside the physical (if not the conceptual) scope of the paint-

ing. Just above the telltale mirror (which reflects more intense light than the large window, perhaps because it's so concentrated), a Latin inscription attests that *Jan Van Eyck was here,* identifying one of the witnesses as the painter himself. Thus the mirror symbolizes the witness-status of the artist's penetrating eye.

Art that deals with scale abounds in the 20th century, with the eccentric assemblages of Joseph Cornell among the most famous. A painting by the Surrealist René Magritte, *Les valeurs personnelles (Personal Values)* (1952), portrays a dollhouselike bedroom with walls painted to resemble a cloudy sky. What makes us assume that the interior is a dollhouse is the unexpected presence of a gigantic comb, shaving brush, cake of soap, wineglass, and match. It would be well to examine Magritte's work in general. A sense of

UNTITLED (PINK PALACE), Joseph Cornell, c. 1946–48, construction, 10 x 16⁷⁄₁₆ x 3¼ inches. © The Joseph and Robert Cornell Memorial Foundation/Licensed by VAGA, New York, New York. Collection Donald Windham.

miniaturization is found in *The Museum of a Night* (1927) and *The Empty Mask* (1928), both paintings of shelflike compartments filled with objects or words.

The effect of mixing scales is disconcerting, shocking, and amusing. Giorgio de Chirico, another visual wit and a forerunner of the Surrealists, composed human torsos of roofs and columns in both his paintings and sculptures. He was fascinated with the conceptual ambiguities of "interior" and "exterior," as in his enigmatic *The House within the House* (1924) and *Temple in the Room* (1967), whose subject is scale.

Many artists work today in small scale. Charles Simonds's miniature clay village, *Dwellings* (1981) is installed in the stairwell of the Whitney Museum in New York. Miriam Schapiro's groundbreaking dollhouse created as a work of fine art is in the collection of the National Museum of American Art, Washington, D.C. Every museum I've seen, anywhere in the world, includes art in miniature scale.

As for me, after a formal education in the liberal and fine arts, I moved to New York City where I painted for fifteen years. My fixed idea was that art was either painting or sculpture, and the bigger the better, which was the predilection of the '70s. Then, one day I accidentally "discovered" the miniature construction, and knew instantly that what I'd stumbled on was a great new genre for making art.

At the time, I'd been rereading *Jane Eyre* with growing obsession, until finally I had an urge to make art based on the novel. I thought this would appease my fixation—cure one obsession with another. I began with a series of big oil paintings that were strong, even torrid, but I wasn't satisfied. Something was missing, and

I was pretty sure it had to do with the medium. So I swung in the opposite direction and made a series of intimate, respectable little watercolors. Still I wasn't happy. I was sure there must be some way to conjure the reverberations of Charlotte Brontë's vision as filtered through my subjective response. If only I could somehow *see* the rooms palpably, if I could in some way *make* them, fake them, manifest them dimensionally, then maybe I'd understand what elusive thing I was after and where to go from there.

Having never owned dollhouses or had any particular interest in them, I was unaware that quite a few shops existed where you could buy almost anything true-to-life in one-inch scale. I simply assumed that everything I needed had to be made from scratch, probably a saving grace, as it literally forced my hand! And so one day in 1986, before I knew what I was doing, I'd put together a semblance of furniture from whatever junk was lying about. I managed to make a wing chair and a fireplace with a volatile little blaze made from the prismatic scrapings of my painting palette. In a stationery store I found a pair of library globes (in an English drawing room they always seem to come in pairs), which began life as cut-rate pencil sharpeners, made in China. Once I'd accumulated some furniture, all propriety fled, along with my lifelong veneration of bound volumes—I swept said books off their shelf, and breathlessly arranged my furniture on it.

Instantly I was excited by the spatial relationships contained by that shelf, which now really did seem like a room. But how to disguise its bookshelfness? Rummaging about in a clutter of ornate

papers, I salvaged some hand-printed wrapping paper embossed with gold, which would do momentarily, I thought, as wallpaper. I taped it on the shelf's three sides and suddenly they became walls. Amazing! The decorative paper also suggested the overblown, ponderous *sense* of an opulent Victorian chamber. This was no stopgap measure, I realized: This was it!

Before long, that shelf became a veritable Victorian drawing room stocked with handmade, recycled, and found items. When the drawing room was done I transformed more shelves into other rooms of Thornfield Hall. By the time I'd finished, I was thrilled because I'd

achieved, in an entirely new way, precisely what I was after: no slavish emulation, but a strong expression of my own.

Those early shelf tableaux mark the beginning of my working in miniature. I'm still at it, as exhilarated as I was by the first one. The medium is inexhaustible, as creative as painting, sculpting, printmaking, and making unique books. For the creative mind, the miniature can compress a salient moment of awareness in a few inches, just as haiku compresses a complete world in a few syllables. In short, there seems to be a universal human desire to yoke the finite to the infinite, the human to the divine, and the breviary moment to eternity.

THORNFIELD HALL, 1986. 10 X 23 X 9 inches. *My first dioramas were rooms based on the novel* Jane Eyre *by Charlotte Brontë. Built into a bookcase, the sitting room fireplace was made from sumi-ink sticks, an antique book cover, and a glass box. The pictures are postage stamps.*

PART I
GETTING STARTED

❧

TO SEE A WORLD IN A GRAIN OF SAND

"If we wish to make a new world we have the material ready. The first one, too, was made out of chaos."

—ROBERT QUILLEN, cited in *Chaos in Wonderland* by Clifford A. Pickover

LITTLE BY LITTLE

I always say: to get started, start getting! Materials, that is. Actually, you need very little to begin creating miniature scenes—some cardboard or a box, tape and glue, an X-Acto knife, and a few pieces of furniture from found objects. You could begin by making your own cardboard diorama, cutting out windows and doors, and arranging walls. For that purpose, I keep a supply of Masonite or foam core rectangles in various dimensions, which I use to work out spaces by propping the panels against bricks or books. When the configuration feels right, I build a box or have one made, using the Masonite or foam core mock-up as a model. This method also allows me to determine how much furniture I might use, as well as their size and placement.

When Alan Wolfson begins one of his complex, multi-layered scenes, he makes a list of ten things he wants to accomplish, and then quits, because he could go on detailing his scenes forever. He says that planning a scene is much like dressing a stage set, including the lighting. David Malcolm Rose photographs his subjects, makes architectural drawings, and then builds his minutely detailed structures inside Plexiglas.

I go about beginning a project without much preparation. Often I get a container first, then acquire one impressive component, like a piece of machinery or

PENNSYLVANIA AVE. ELEVATED, Alan Wolfson, 1995. 11 x 14⅜ x 17 inches. Courtesy Bernarducci Meisel Gallery, New York. *The scene is an elevated train station. The track cross ties are wood, and the tracks are from a model railroad. The front grille on the train (the accordion gate) is soldered brass.*

an exquisite chair, which serves as the catalyst to build an entire scene. The springboard for *Portrait of Wendy as a Room* was a celadon-green chair purchased from a miniatures store.

Sometimes I start with an idea or theme, and then look for materials that suit it. To help me get started, I keep a large carton full of intriguing and inspiring objects. When I began the series of twelve

miniature sets for Mozart's opera *The
Magic Flute,* the first thing I did was put
on a CD of the opera. As the overture
began, I became overwhelmed by the
greatness of the music. Where would
I start? How could I start? How could I
accomplish such an ambitious project?
With my mind a total blank, I went rummaging in the catchall carton—and a
miracle happened. Just as Papageno began
trilling on his panpipe, my hand, as if on
cue, closed round an 80¢ plastic panpipe.
I promptly began to accompany the bird-
catcher—I, who can't sing a straight line,
was now participating in an opera!

Taking this event as a sign, I went
in search of real panpipes to use as a gate
for what would become *Papageno's Nest.*
I found bamboo panpipes quickly enough,
and continued my "shopping" in local
flea markets. Soon I came upon an
antique wooden flute, which matched the
libretto's description of the magic flute.
Okay, I thought, *here's the flute. Now
where's the magic?* I turned around: there
was a huge sign with MAGIC spelled out
in four-foot high red letters. Shortly after
that I found fancy gilt picture frames,
the solution for the stages—they'd make
rococo prosceniums!

INSPIRATIONS

Often I am asked where my ideas come from. A proper answer to that would be a book in itself. Ideas come from simply looking around on long walks. Big cities are rife with visual stimulation. I appreciate the energy of graffiti, the billboards and signage—the eyesores most people avoid. I love traffic cones, manhole tents, loading docks, scaffolding, and construction sites; the harmony within the cacophony.

Other sources of inspiration come from museums and art galleries. Frequently I'll see some theme or application from large-scale art that strikes me as transposable into miniature scale. I've always been tremendously inspired by music and literature. I also love sets from theater, television, and movies—anything theatrical, stage-like, pretend.

Of course, materials in and of themselves are immediately inspirational. About ten years ago I made a miniature loading dock out of a splinter from a real loading dock. I was impressed by how much alike they were—the large piece of wood and its fragment. I thought of examples in nature of such reduplication: branches replicating trees and rocks imitating mountains, how a patch of moss resembles a meadow, and a fern leaf seems made up of miniature ferns.

HIDDEN LIBRARY, 1990. 14 x 23 x 9 inches. *I recently became interested in Feng Shui, the ancient art of arranging rooms. According to Feng Shui, one shouldn't cram books into shelves without leaving some "breathing" space. Working in miniature, I can apply these and other "decorating" principles, or aim in the opposite direction. To express congestion and claustrophobia, I cram the bookshelves full!*

Opposite:

FELISSIMO TOWNHOUSE, 1993.
50 x 30 x 19 inches. *I made
two Felissimo townhouses:
The first was for the store's
Christmas window, the second
was commissioned as a permanent display in the Osaka,
Japan, airport.*

BELOW THE CITY, 1990.
17 x 30 x 11¼ inches. *My first
subway station was built into
a bookcase. Nothing is glued
down; all the elements remain
changeable. The token booth is
an electrical box; the clock, a
wristwatch; the gates, heater-
filters; the girders, shelf brackets. The PA speakers are sink
aerators; the tunnels, antique
orthodontia molds. The ceiling
is embellished cove-molding.*

PICK OF
THE LITTER

I generally get what I need by hunting
and gathering. I hunt for specific items,
and gather likely things for future use.
It's been my experience that *if you look
hard enough, you'll always find what you
need.* You may be surprised to chance
upon something you hadn't first considered, but that will work better than your
initial idea. Early on, when beginning
Below the City, I was stumped about what
to do for subway turnstiles. Just as I was
about to register for a course in soldering
or welding, I found a ready-made answer
in the form of a disposable lighter. I
prefer not to repeat solutions, so instead

of using the same plastic lighters again
for subsequent subways, I made turnstiles
out of metal lighters and breath mint
containers.

Another spectacular "find" happened
when I got a commission to create, exclu-
sively out of found and recycled objects,
the Christmas window for Felissimo, a
beautiful shop in midtown Manhattan.
My idea was to replicate the entire four-
story building, plus a slice of wintry
Central Park. Immediately, I found a discarded toy chalkboard leaning against the
chain-link fence of a parking lot. The
chalkboard was the perfect size, shape,
structure, and even color for Felissimo's
bronze-green mansard roof. I used this
lucky find to determine the dimensions
of the entire building.

MATERIALS AND COMPONENTS

A friend recently showed me a Japanese TV documentary about a miniature-making competition. There were two parts to this competition: replicating real buildings, and making up imaginary ones. First each contestant selected a shop—a tea house, a sushi restaurant, etc. Then, with a stopwatch running, they sat in front of their subjects and reproduced the buildings exactly in miniature, using only foam core, paper, wood, rulers, blades, and glue. With these limited materials they were able to simulate bricks, concrete, stone, chopsticks, delicious-looking food, tables and chairs, signs, and foliage. Next, as the audience watched, the contestants made their imaginary scenes. One was a house where a murder took place—you could see the imprint of the body on the floor, trampled flowers, muddy footprints on the ladder rungs leading to the bedroom, and other clues—all built from scratch, right before our eyes!

This book doesn't limit materials to foam core and cardstock—just about anything goes. Alan Wolfson scratch-builds everything primarily from plastics like polystyrene and acrylic, supplemented with some metal and wood. He makes every phone, hydrant, sink, sign, and joist, not to mention each individually cut, painted, and glued-down styrene brick.

Miniaturists make use of all sorts of interesting materials, with an emphasis on transforming found, recycled, and mass-produced objects. Barbara Minch swathes filigreed metal and crenellated cardboard onto armatures of Styrofoam packing. She then details the constructions with a multiplicity of jewelry findings that serve as architectural ornamentation. Some artists use dollhouse furniture that's been carefully altered, distressed, disguised, and manipulated into new distinction. I've used toys, game parts, and machinery parts in several pieces.

With an experimental attitude and an open mind, you'll discover that almost anything can be used in a miniature. As you keep working, you'll find that the success of a scene depends on the appropriateness of its components. Every element in a piece should serve a purpose and contribute to the whole. One pitfall is to indiscriminately include distracting extras unrelated to the composition or intention of a work. John Mackiewicz warns us against the temptation of "showcasing" elements that were expensive or hard to make. Bury it, or at least obscure it, he says; there's no reason to reveal cost or effort to the viewer. Backstage secrets and magicians' tricks should not be divulged.

SHOPPING

As you begin working in miniature, it's helpful to have basic tools, supplies, and materials at hand. Here are some things you might want to get from various retailers.

ELECTRICAL STORES

Strip lighting
Extension cord(s)

STATIONERY STORES

Laminating sheets (for framing pictures and laminating miniature postcards)
Liquid Paper® (correction fluid)
Metallic pens: silver, gold, and copper
Rubber bands and adhesive tape (to hold components while gluing)
Paper clamps (also called "binder clips")

Triangle and cork-backed metal ruler
Double-stick tape and regular Scotch tape
Patterned giftwrap paper (for wallpaper)
Small self-adhesive notepads (to make books, pads, and for labeling parts of a construction)
Index cards in various colors
Buff-colored card stock (for making miniature file folders)
Compact hand-held stapler (to secure tiny hems for basting; for miniature legal pads, etc.)

HARDWARE STORES

Wood stain and finish (various shades)
Spray paint: black, white, and gray primer
Drill (for holes for electrical wires)

Jigsaw (to cut hard wood)
Razor saw, coping saw, straight saw (any of these)
Tin snips
Needlenose and regular pliers
Small hammer
Screwdrivers: regular and Philips head (in different sizes)
Small nails and brads
Fine sandpaper
L-shaped corner mending braces (to use as right-angles)
3-inch paint rollers (optional; to paint surfaces like walls)
Small-size sponge brushes (also available in art stores)
Plastic multi-drawer utility bins
Disposable aluminum pans and Styrofoam® trays (in which to paint and glue components)
PVA glue (such as Weldbond®)
Epoxy glue
Spackling compound

Lightweight chicken wire (to make armatures)

SCALE MODEL SUPPLIERS

Spongy foam foliage and lichen
Rolls and/or packages of "grass"
Trees (try making these yourself: see "Landscaping," pages 114–122)
Liquid solvent/cement for plastics
Assorted basswood and balsa strips; baseboard, chair rail, cornice, banister, dentil molding, picture-frame strips, etc. (dollhouse stores also carry these)
1/16-inch Plexiglas: clear (for windows); opaque, white, and smoky (for building facades, and to make ponds and lakes)
Plastic cutter
Styrene strips and sheets
Sheets of plastic mirror

MORE SHOPPING

ARTS AND CRAFTS STORES

Disposable hobby brushes

Marine sponges (for wall treatments)

X-Acto knife and blades (#11)

White craft glue (regular and extra-tacky)

Aerosol or "spray mount" adhesive (a good substitute for dollhouse wallpaper gel; great for landscaping)

Matte and gloss waterbase sealer

Small jars of waterbase hobby or craft paints in wide assortment of colors

Acrylic gloss varnish (good for making "snow" glisten; applied with a brush, it's easier to manage than aerosols)

Small wood plaques (for table tops and "plaster" ceiling medallions and molding)

Foam core (assortment of sizes, 1/16 inch thick)

Papier-mâché (or similar modeling material like Cell-U-Clay®)

Crackle® medium (to weather and age painted wood)

Krylon® Crystal Clear (a colorless adhesive spray that makes scenes look wet or damp; also protects color from fading)

Polymer modeling clay (like Fimo® or Sculpey®)

Paste brush (to sweep off table surfaces)

MINIATURES STORES

Quick-Grab® glue

Contact cement (good for vinyl, tiles, plastics, and more)

Wallpaper paste/gel (could use spray-mount)

Miniature mortar mix (to grout terracotta tile or brick; could use spackling compound)

Sticky-wax (temporarily sticks things down)

Miniature miter box (for picture frames, ceiling molding, and floorboards)

Readymade dollhouse accessories and roomboxes

Lighting kits

COFFEE SHOPS

Plastic spoons and knives (to use as tools)

Single-serving creamer containers (for lampshades, waste baskets, and to mix small amounts of paint)

Plastic and aluminum take-out containers (for mixing paint)

Flexible drinking straws (for rainspouts, interior pipes, desk-lamp necks)

DRUGSTORES

Nail clippers (to trim wood strips)

Tweezers (to hold small things steady or to help glue down tiny things)

Emory boards (to sand thin wood strips)

Hairspray (to set pleats in fabric)

Round or rectangular satin-trimmed powder puffs (for cushions)

Small cosmetic sponges (to sponge-paint surfaces; creates a mottled effect)

Small cosmetic mirrors

PET SUPPLY STORES

Cat litter (for gravel)

Plastic aquarium plants (for foliage)

Aquarium gravel in various colors

An aquarium (to build in)

SEWING STORES

Braided trims and ribbons

Fabrics

Buttons

Pearl-headed straight pins

Button-covering kits (to make cushions)

Nylon strapping (available in many colors—brown and tan look like straw. The weave is perfect for baskets, hampers, and hats.)

GROCERY STORES

Sandwich bags (to collect specimens and sort tiny things)

Aluminum pans (for the glue bath and to catch paint drips)

Wooden crates

Dried chili flakes (for autumnal ground cover)

Herbs (for topiaries and other foliage)

THRIFT SHOPS, FLEA MARKETS, GARAGE SALES

Jewelry findings

Small boxes

Beads, baubles, and buttons

Wooden blocks, dominoes, dice, and old board games

Whatever else attracts your attention!

REMEMBRANCE OF THINGS CLASSED

Paradoxically, one needs *a lot* of carefully organized space when working in small scale. Materials do accumulate, along with empty boxes, equipment, and finished art. I try to keep my studio in reasonable order, but do have a separate, small room designated a "wreck room" that I don't even try to tame. It's good to be discriminating about what you keep around. My general rule is that if I haven't used something in a year, out it goes.

Don't be surprised if friends, hearing of your ventures, are suddenly galvanized to clean out attics and basements and bombard you with the results of their purges: accretions of charms, spindles, toy soldiers, dollhouse furniture, game pieces, guitar picks. One friend periodically mails me a jar full of trinkets. Another recently sent a shoebox of antique lace and rickrack. A third shipped her grandmother's lifelong collection of wooden spools. I have crates brimming with Legos® and other blocks donated by well-meaning amigos. (Legos, by the way, are great for building facades, as in *The Temple of Wisdom*, shown on page 117.)

After spending a few years in chaos, I developed the discipline of putting away incoming arrivals and discarding those that seem unusable—things obviously out of scale, too toylike, or outside the scope of my interests or subject matter. A good reason for storing things tidily is that you can find something when you need it. After all, what's the good of owning a box

CITY OF GLASS, 1994. 4 x 3¼ x 2 inches. *The "glass" is actually plastic building blocks.*

Opposite:
LABORATORY TABLE, 1993. 3 x 6 x 2 inches. Private collection. *An example of reworked commercial dollhouse furniture, in this case a kitchen sink.*

of cerulean blue marbles if you forgot you had them, or can't find them?

I systematize bins and drawers into categories, such as "decorative papers," "wood scraps," "styrene," and "plastic shapes." Sometimes shape dictates the classification: "circles," "blocks," "sticks." At times, I further specify with labels marked "gems," "flexible straws," "hearing-aid batteries." Methods of organization are as individual as signatures. After "pirating" dozens of plastic model kits for their parts, John Mackiewicz separates and classifies them by shape rather than by their intended function, and stores them in parts-drawers.

From hardware stores you can get multi-drawer bins convenient for grouping together small items; they hold a lot and stack compactly. I also have metal cabinets

ANN'S CALLIGRAPHY STUDIO, 1994. 10 X 14 X 11½ inches. *This is a replica of my mother's studio in Miami. The framed pieces are membership cards to her calligraphy organizations. All the furniture, fixtures, and equipment were made from found objects.*

with small drawers for notions, findings, pegs, tiny doors, windows, trusses, and the like. Flat files, or ordinary dressers with large drawers, hold paper, slide sheets, drawings, and other things that should be kept flat. You might want to have a rolling taboret (there's a miniature one in *Ann's Calligraphy Studio)* (above) for portable access to paints and small tools.

Of course, a well-stocked, well-organized studio saves time and money. I was

Here's a sample of using a slide sheet to keep little pictures visible, accessible, and ordered.

able to make the bed vignette on page 98 almost as fast as making a real bed, because everything in the scene was at hand. The fireplace room on page 107, which also came together in a twinkling, was assembled from things I had too.

In a separate file cabinet I keep folders for art reproductions, pictures of clock and watch faces, miniature pictures of magazines and newspapers (from advertisements), tiny photos (from snapshots and catalogs), inspiring interiors and architecture (from design magazines), and articles about miniatures. To stow tiny pictures, I use plastic slide sheets (left).

It's important to document your finished pieces, especially if you plan to exhibit and sell your work. I always have slides taken of my projects. I label each slide with title, date, and dimensions.

SEVEN HABITS OF
HIGHLY EFFECTIVE MINIATURISTS

1. When shopping or foraging, carry a small metal tape measure (the kind that retracts into a coil) until you develop a knack for assessing size and scale. Remember to bring it with you to flea markets and garage sales!

2. Carry one or two plastic bags to put street-findings in—but be careful what you pick up. (Often, I've impulsively lunged for certain dangerous items, like the shattered wind-shield glass in *Loading Dock with Drain Pipe* [above]. You might consider carrying a pair of disposable gloves.)

3. Carry a notebook to jot ideas or sketches, or the locations of places you'd like to return to. Bring along a camera to take pictures of scenes that you might want to re-create in miniature.

4. Stay organized— clean up as you work, and put everything away, no matter how tempting to leave a jumble of supplies for the next day. This is especially important if you're working on more than one project at a time.

5. Don't overlook *anything* small-scale—magazine ads, junk jewelry, plastic aquarium plants, packaging, disposable material. (*Rough House* [below] was made from the ripped-up cardboard backing of a discarded fabric-sample book.)

6. Window shop. Ideas can come from every kind of window-dressing, including the small windows reserved for jewelry displays. Windows are, after all, glass boxes.

7. Haunt the museums! Study great art from all ages for composition and color, and for inspiration.

Collect postcards and art books. Look especially for painters of interiors, like Valadon, Vuillard, Vermeer, Van Eyck, Van Gogh . . . and those are just some of the Vs!

Above:
LOADING DOCK WITH DRAIN PIPE, 1991. 10 X 14 X 3¼ inches. *Note the cracked windshield glass. Container is a heavy wooden box from an antiques store.*

Left:
ROUGH HOUSE, 2001. 4½ X 5 X 4½ inches. *While tearing apart a fabric-sample pad, the cardboard automatically configured itself to resemble a house. The nails kept the thick pile of fabrics together.*

A ROOMBOX OF ONE'S OWN

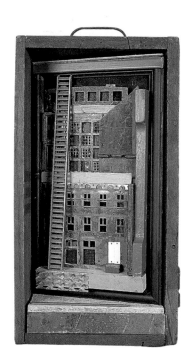

What a frame is to a picture, a box is to a construction. Containers protect their contents, define an artwork's boundaries, provide visual focus, and render a work portable. If you're not ready to commit a scene to a separate box just yet, you might build into a bookcase as I did, which costs nothing and takes up no space. Using what's at hand will help break the ice and nudge you towards making that initial investment in a container.

When I finally outgrew the habit of furnishing bookcases with subways and fantasy-chambers, I reshelved my tottering library stacks and considered other possibilities. I had neither carpentry skills nor power tools, so building boxes wasn't an option. Instead, I began scouting local flea markets for boxes. With a little imagination, you can figure out all sorts of ways to enclose a miniature scene! Among the many inexpensive boxes I found were a metal utility box, World War II ammo box (left), stereo box, fan box, and clock cases (below).

Even more ideas were beginning to spring up. From a plastics store, I bought scores of small, economical boxes. I saved and recycled matchboxes (opposite, top) and tin lozenge boxes, and "pirated" (to

Above:

SHAFTWAY, 1992. 15 x 8 x 4 inches. *This piece is built into a World War I ammunition box. Found containers often suggest subjects to build in them. The dense, battered exterior and height of the ammo box reminded me of an elevator shaftway.*

Right:

CLOCK TOWER GARRETT, 1991. 13 x 8½ x 5 inches. *This fantasy of an artist's digs was built into a clock case. The dominating clock face reads as a rose window.*

Two matchbox containers, 1991.

NEST, Diane Price, 1998. 9 x 6¾ x 6 inches. *The cigar box lid becomes an angled wall and creates a top opening to let in more light. The door can be closed.*

use John Mackiewicz's term) Russian lacquered boxes. I even used a square wooden saki cup, and installed a vertical urban triptych in a medicine cabinet. Other containers were produce crates (free from the grocers'). I also rediscovered the beauty of cigar boxes, which I could have from smoke shops for a few dollars. One inspiration is *Nest*, Diane Price's almost gymnastic reconstruction of a cigar box into a room with irregular walls (right).

With a little inventiveness, a variety of everyday materials can be transformed into unusual containers. A cousin gave me a pair of five-inch shower-door handles that I turned into subway platforms (page 1). Among my own possessions I rediscovered my father's medical light-box, in which I built a streetscape (page 34). Discarded desks were plentiful from the streets; I hauled their drawers back to my studio and in them built storefronts with projecting display windows, an opera set after Puccini's *Turandot* (page 32), and other scenes. (I keep several drawers empty to use for gathering and sorting materials for new projects.)

Recently I was visiting friends who have a beautiful library with a nonworking Victorian fireplace. The fire screen was gone that day, and for the first time

I could see the curved black aperture. "A rococo garden," I said, in the middle of a sentence about something else. "What?" asked my mystified hosts. "The fireplace," I explained. "There should be a rococo garden in it." "You're right," my friends agreed, and without further discussion, I returned a few weeks later and built *Fireplace Garden* (below).

Fireplaces are only one unusual container in which to create a miniature environment. Consider using an aquarium or terrarium, placed upright or on its side. You might explore art supply stores for shadow boxes and deep picture frames, and housewares stores for finished wood utensil boxes with ledgelike edges that could support a Plexiglas cover.

Opposite:
TURANDOT, 1997. 20 X 23 X 24 inches. *Opera, with its fantasy, hyperbole, color, and stage design, lends itself well to miniaturization. I built this set for Puccini's opera inside a curved desk drawer. (Joan Ann Mrazik, who is known for her realistic dollhouse baked goods, made the heads of the hapless princes.)*

FIREPLACE GARDEN, 1999. Courtesy Gail Levin and John B. Van Sickle. *A miniature rococo garden built into a non-working Victorian fireplace. The top of the garden table is a drink coaster. The statue is a plastic cake decoration, sprayed gray. The base of the statue is the top of a laundry detergent bottle. The fence ornaments are oxidized brass place-card holders. The miniature scrapbook is meant to hold photos of the owners.*

CREATING A ROOMBOX

If you wish to make your own roomboxes, you can do so with a few simple tools and materials: a jigsaw, straight or coping saw; ½" or ¼" fiberboard or plywood; wood screws; hammer and nails; white glue; and sandpaper. Easy instructions for building boxes, including templates, can be adapted from birdhouse-building books. Then follow these basic steps to transform your box into a miniature room.

1. Prime the ceiling with waterbased latex flat paint and sand it lightly until smooth.

2. *If wiring for electricty:* Install wiring tape by pressing and smoothing it across the walls and ceilings. Dab tape on the ceiling with latex flat paint.

3. Give the entire ceiling another coat of waterbased latex flat or semigloss paint (flat paint hides the wiring tape better).

4. *If using terracotta tile floors:* Install terracotta tile floors with extra-tacky white craft glue. When dry, grout with miniature mortar. Be sure to scrub the tiles thoroughly before the mortar dries, otherwise the tiles will have a cloudy appearance.

5. *Wallpapering:* If you haven't installed the window and door yet, hold off for a bit. If the window and door can be detached without damage to the roombox, do that now. Put up wallpaper with wallpaper paste or gel. If possible, wallpaper completely over the empty window- and doorholes and allow the wallpaper to dry thoroughly. When the wallpaper is dry, cut out the window and door openings with an X-Acto knife.

6. Put down carpeting or plastic tile floor with tacky glue. If wood floors are to be installed, stain and/or varnish them and allow them to dry before gluing them into the box. Glue down wood floors with Quick-Grab glue (see "Shopping," page 26).

7. Paint, stain, and/or varnish doors, baseboards, window moldings, and ceiling moldings. Allow all pieces to dry before gluing them into place with Quick-Grab glue.

8. Install ceiling fixtures, such as a working chandelier, available in miniature shops.

9. Paint, stain, and/or varnish stairs and allow them to dry before gluing them into the box.

Thanks to Renée McKenna, Katharine Forsyth, Eric Edelman, and Abigayl Sperber for this guidance.

HOPE (SCAFFOLDING), 1991. 11 x 14¼ x 3½ inches. Private collection. *This vignette is composed of metal umbrella spokes, corrugated cardboard, and other found objects arranged in a light-box.*

LET THERE
BE LIGHT!

"And there was light." If only it were so simple! There are many options for bringing light into a roombox. The effort is worth it, for any miniature scene is greatly enhanced by illumination. Lighting serves two purposes: all-over illumination for visibility, and accent lights for atmosphere. Any kind of electric light can be duplicated in miniature, including incandescent, fluorescent, neon, chase lights, and fiber optics.

Though electrification isn't impossibly difficult, I tend to avoid wiring my dioramas, opting for other solutions. Generally, I use strip lighting, a simple, inexpensive alternative to wiring a box. Electrical stores carry these "shelf" or "accent" lights, which come in different lengths (10", 20", 30") and their housing in black, white, chrome, etc. You can mount the strip on any surface of the interior of your box—vertically, horizontally, diagonally, or across the ceiling. The swiveling bulb casing allows the aim of the light to be adjusted. To diminish brightness, I baffle strip lights with packing

DENTIST, 1939, John Mackiewicz, 1994. 10 x 14 x 12 inches. *The source of information for this scene was a reference book of dental offices through the ages. Mackiewicz made the chair, drill station, spittoon, and X-ray machine from scratch, using hundreds of parts from kits. In contrast to the stark, terrifying-looking machinery and the eerily averted position of the chair, the waiting room glows with an inviting ambience beyond.*

MISS AMERICA DINER, Alan Wolfson, 2000. 13 x 17½ x 18¼ inches. Photo: Bill Dow. *This restaurant is based on a diner in Jersey City. Wolfson has an elaborate visual narrative going on in a spot that's usually overlooked—the roof.*

tape, as in *Steamship* (page 59). Here the strip is concealed behind a ceiling beam. In one work, I mounted a pair of the lights vertically, on either side of the box, so that one or both sides can be illuminated at any given time.

John Mackiewicz's lighting strategies are complex and ingenious. He uses three sets of animated lights, all LEDs (light emitting diodes) connected to an electronic chip that gives the effect of animation. He uses full-size fluorescent fixtures that have been diffused and tinted with colored gels. Sometimes he uses the miniature incandescent lights half-strength (6 rather than 12 volts), to add a moody dimness to a scene. In *Dentist*, 1939 (page 35), the front room's stark, cold brightness comes from a fluorescent bulb covered

with blue gel. In contrast, the waiting room beyond looks warm and inviting due to the incandescent lights. For overall illumination, Mackiewicz uses fluorescent bulbs from nine to thirteen inches long, hidden in the casing at the top of the box. He feels that a piece should have enough autonomous light to allow it to be shown in any setting. When the lights are off in his dioramas, the artful weathering and highlighting seem as exaggerated as stage makeup; when the lights are on, the illusion balances into perfect realism.

Alan Wolfson too has a sophisticated, experimental approach to lighting. In *Miss America Diner* (above) he used a new type of lighting made from LEDs to simulate spotlights under the stainless steel apron and above each window. He made a miniature fluorescent fixture out of a 3⁄16" tube. By using fiber optics, one can create the illusion of thousands of light bulbs with a single power source. Wolfson once made a casino with 2,500 exterior chase lights.

Light can be manipulated to create a certain mood or ambience. Susan Leopold uses indirect light to create mystery in night scenes and tranquility in day scenes. In *Trepidation* (right) the fluorescent ceiling fixture is actually a plastic box that receives light from a fluorescent bulb mounted in the top. In *Pyramid Lanterns* (below) the glass lanterns receive their light from a fluorescent bulb mounted under the floor. Holes in the floor under each lantern siphon the light into the lanterns. There are no lights at all in *Jnaneshwar's Dream* (page 48). For illumination, the scene depends on ambient light filtered through a sheet of blue

acetate mounted in the ceiling. This underwater-blueness could have been achieved with gel-covered bulbs—but I decided to go *au natural*.

TREPIDATION, Susan Leopold, 1989. 16 x 36 x 15 inches. Courtesy of Jean Albano Gallery, Chicago, Illinois. *This is a Lens-Box mixed-media construction (one of four lens views). Leopold manipulates her models, using forced perspective, shifting scales, and the qualities of the lens itself, to create a sense of claustrophobia and alienation.*

PYRAMID LANTERNS (TUNNEL BELOW SUBWAY) from THE MAGIC FLUTE series, 1997–99. 19 x 26½ x 14 inches. *An artist who works in glass made the lanterns, which are illuminated by a fluorescent bulb hidden under the floor. The light comes up through holes beneath each pyramid.*

TAPEWIRING

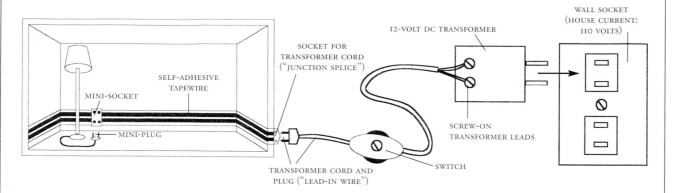

WALL SOCKET
(HOUSE CURRENT:
110 VOLTS)

12-VOLT DC TRANSFORMER

SOCKET FOR
TRANSFORMER CORD
("JUNCTION SPLICE")

SELF-ADHESIVE
TAPEWIRE

MINI-SOCKET

MINI-PLUG

SCREW-ON
TRANSFORMER LEADS

SWITCH

TRANSFORMER CORD AND
PLUG ("LEAD-IN WIRE")

DIAGRAM FOR AN ELECTRIFIED ROOMBOX. Roombox and components are not drawn to scale.

If you're feeling in the dark about all this lighting technology, don't blow a fuse. Eric Edelman gives instructions below on how to light a roombox *simply*. He says: "You can easily electrify your roomboxes with 12-volt dollhouse lighting kits, which are based on using 'tapewire,' a self-adhesive tape with two tracks of copper foil (see illustrations). Tapewiring systems offer many advantages:

- They're easy and quick to use. (A typical layout is shown in the illustration above.)

- Tapewire is thin enough to hide beneath wallpaper or a coat of paint. Its plastic surface is treated to receive water-based paint, and its edges may be sanded invisibly against the wall.

- Few components are required: the tapewire, a "junction splice" socket, a transformer cord (lead-in wire) with a plug, on-off switch, screw-on transformer leads, and a 12-volt transformer. Lamps, bulbs, ceiling lights, etc. connect to the system with small brass nails, brass eyelets, or miniature plug-and-socket combinations sold separately.

- After the initial installation, tapewire layouts can be expanded. The layout in the illustration shows a single strip of tapewire with a miniature floor lamp plugged into a wall-socket mounted on the wire. If you wished to put in a ceiling light later, you could add a second tapewire strip running onto the ceiling, connected to the main tapewire. (But to keep the new tape hidden, it must be added before the wall is papered or painted.)

- Tapewire systems work well with all 12-volt miniature lighting accessories: plugs, sockets, "bare bulbs" (see Katharine Forsyth's *Bathroom*, page 101), fluorescent bulbs ("fluorettes"), sconces, ceiling fixtures, and lamps.

- Tapewire is reliable, especially when installed as a continuous run.

- With tapewire, you can achieve all sorts of effects. For a twilight atmosphere, conceal miniature bulbs behind a translucently painted dawn or dusk background with tapewire on the exterior of the roombox.

Cir-Kit Concepts, Inc. makes a line of 12-volt dollhouse tapewire lighting kits, available through dollhouse and hobby shops. Be sure to avoid buying single-foil tapewire kits, which are difficult to install and inferior to the double tapewire kits.

SETTING
THE STAGE

I think it's always advantageous to shield a miniature with glass or Plexiglas. One reason is to keep out dust. Dust is simply the wrong scale—and if you let a miniature scene get dusty, it will just look dusty.

Of course it's always easier to keep dust out of a box than to try to spruce it up later with a feather-duster, hair-dryer, or hand-held vacuum. (If your scene calls for dust, you should simulate grime, perhaps with diluted brown and/or black waterbased paint—see "Distressing News," page III.)

There's a psychological advantage to having a transparent front. Without jeopardizing the "come hither" signals a compelling miniature evokes, a clear front telegraphs "hands off," and asserts a subtle threshold to your make-believe world—like the wardrobe in C. S. Lewis's Narnia books, or the rabbit hole in *Alice in Wonderland*. Things behind glass are alluringly elusive, like treasures in museum vitrines and the mysterious, inviting autonomy of fish tanks.

When I finally discovered dollhouse stores, I bought readymade roomboxes, which usually come with removable Plexiglas fronts. The disadvantage of these affordable boxes is their limited dimensions and proportions. Squashing my scenes into the same configurations soon became tedious: I didn't want to make another 10 x 15 x 9 inch diorama!

From the beginning, I regarded my little scenes as stage sets and preferred boxes with oddly angled walls. To escape

the straight and static confines of store-bought boxes, I resorted to hiring carpenters to build boxes to my specs. This costly enterprise was justified because of the importance of containers, and their power to contribute to or detract from a scene's effectiveness. For *The Magic Flute* series (see throughout), I had a woodworker build half-inch-thick mahogany stages with curved floors, flaring walls, and intricate proscenia. Another series I had containers built for was *Hiding Places* (above). While the walls seem uniform, they subtly taper inward at the back.

HIDING PLACES, 1996. *Four stacked tenement rooms, two with bathrooms, each 13½ x 12 x 19 inches.*

FORTUNE STAR RESTAURANT,
FRONT AND BACK VIEWS, 1993,
14 X 20 X 10 inches. Private
collection. *Modeled after an
actual Chinese restaurant. As
in "Bazzini's" (see Contents,
page 7), the relatively serious
façade contrasts with the
whimsically festive rear.*

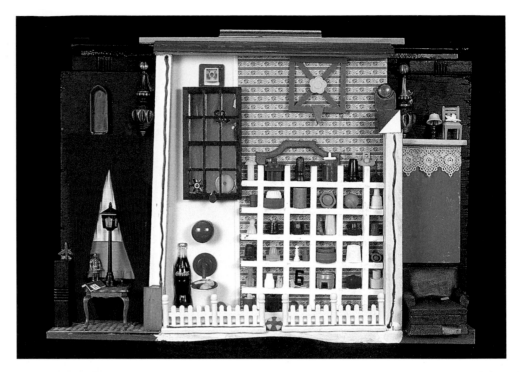

UNBOXED MINIATURES

Not all miniatures are consigned to boxes. Barbara Minch's *All That Glitters Is Not Gold* (page 24) is a wall-relief. Tim Prythero's monumental *14th and Union* (below) is freestanding. I've made pieces that stand on wooden carving-board bases; freestanding loading-dock structures; and sprawling tableaux so large in scope that I had to take them apart for lack of room to keep them (see *Medieval Hall*, page 90).

For freeform, sculptural settings like *Gizmos (Rube Goldberg Variations)* (page 43), a right-angled box would have stifled the eccentric biomorphic impression I wanted. The curving shell lodging that piece, as well as *Breakfast Below* (page 42), were sculpted from papier-mâché, supported by an armature of chicken-wire.

Some dioramas are freestanding and designed to be viewed front-and-back or in the round. In some of the front-and-back works, the two sides contrast as radically as a manic-depressive personality! The façade of *Bazzini's* is a sober representation of an actual Tribeca building. Its reverse, however, borders on the riotous (Contents, page 7). The front of *Fortune Star Restaurant* (opposite) is a faithful portrait of a real building, graffiti included; but the back looks like the site of a hallucinogenic tea party.

The largest 360-degree diorama I ever made was a miniature television studio called *Catherine's Place*, inspired by the TV series *Beauty and the Beast*. I was attracted to the underlying theme: the fragile interconnection of two mutually exclusive worlds. I began by constructing a bird's-eye view of the opulent apartment and elevator lobby, all under a removable roof. Around the periphery are departments of a film studio: Wardrobe,

14TH AND UNION, Tim Prythero, 1990. 57 x 29½ x 34 inches. Photo © Gerald Peters. Courtesy O.K. Harris Works of Art, New York. *Prythero began this piece by building a model, then allowed the work to evolve during construction.*

Matte Painting, Props, Wardrobe, Carpentry, and Craft Service. Another construction, *Hiding Places* (page 39), extends this theme in its portrayal of the simultaneous existence of diverse realities, represented by four rooms stacked like a tenement; the details reveal the biographical facts of four discrete solitaries.

Above:

GIZMOS, 1992. 21 X 25¼ X 17 inches. *This fantasy underground apartment-laboratory is housed in a shell made from papier-mâché and chicken wire.*

Left:

L-SHAPED BUILDING, 1991. 17 X 20 X 4 inches. Collection of the Museum of the City of New York. *A freestanding piece that transcends the limitations of the rectangular box.*

Opposite:

BREAKFAST BELOW, 1992. 22 X 31 X 24 inches. Collection of the Museum of the City of New York. *The splayed roofline of this underground refectory is made from coat hangers. Its curving shape unifies the composition.*

PART II

THE CREATIVE PROCESS

AESTHETIC PRINCIPLES IN MINIATURE

"There is a great beauty in smallness. One gets all the charm of design and colour and effect, because you can see so much more in combination and juxtaposing. . . . The result is a closeness and fineness of texture which please both eye and mind."

—A. C. BENSON, *Everybody's Book of the Queen's Dolls' House,* 1924.

Detail. FLORINE STETTHEIMER, THE BALLROOM, 1996. 12 x 18½ x 8 inches. *Inspired by Florine and Carrie Stettheimer's famous dollhouse, in the collection of The Museum of the City of New York.*

COLOR

ROOM WITH A VIEW,
John Mackiewicz, 1990.
12 x 18 x 14 inches. Courtesy of
O. K. Harris Works of Art,
New York. *This piece was
inspired by Edward Hopper's
painting* Room in Brooklyn.
*The stark interior contrasts with
the complex urban backdrop,
an example of forced perspective.
Mackiewicz used various scale
model building components,
adding more blue-gray paint to
each descending layer.*

I met an astrologer at a party a few years ago. After exchanging chitchat about what we "did," I asked if she could guess my sign. "Leo," she said promptly, and I was floored. "How could you tell?" I asked, a bit spooked—no one had ever guessed my sign. "Easy," she shrugged. "By what you do. You say you build stage-sets out of toys and odds and ends. That would be a perfect Leo occupation—play combined with drama."

What has astrology to do with color, you may be wondering. Well, not very much, but there's a useful analogy here. Just as each astrological sign bears certain traits, and their contradictory aspects, so each hue in the spectrum possesses distinctive and opposing vibrational and emotive qualities. Yellow can seem sunny or sickly; blue, morose or serene; green can imply prosperity or jealousy; red can be read as vital or virulent.

What causes this mercurial connotative range are a color's intensity (saturation) and its degree of lightness or darkness, warmth or coolness. Think of the variations of red from pale pink to deep burgundy, from warm to cool (depending on whether it contains yellow or blue), and from bright (imagine a red tulip in sunlight) to grayed-out (a tulip at twilight). Of equal importance, a color's relationship to its neighboring colors will affect its visual and emotive charge. Here, too, the zodiacal analogy applies: The sun sign is only part of someone's astrological make-up—the

total chart depends on the relationship of the planets in all twelve houses.

The language of color is subjective and personal—perhaps the most expressive element in the visual arts. Everyone has strong opinions and associations about color, which can work toward unique expression. Of the myriad ways to approach color when working in miniature, the following are a few ideas:

If your intention is "realism," colors should be toned down. With diminished scale comes diminished color. John Mackiewicz says that the "grayer" the color, the closer a viewer will approach the piece. In *Room with a View* (opposite), the overall color and tonal effects are muted and lean towards the middle grays, which tend, like a whisper, to draw the viewer inside. Alan Wolfson selects and mixes colors instinctively. He starts with a base coat applied with an airbrush, then keeps building layers of shading until the color seems the "right scale." The bright fluorescent traffic cones in front of *Miss America Diner* (page 36) were toned down to miniature scale.

Bright colors work better in nonrealistic scenes. In *Frida Kahlo* (above) my aim was to re-create the Mexican painter's life using the colors she favored in her paintings. The multihued walls support the theme of her palette and her home, and I made the colors vivid to heighten

FRIDA KAHLO, 1993.
14 X 20 X 13 inches.
Frida Kahlo led a fascinating—dare I say colorful—life, which I wished to express "all at once" through a diorama. The bed, wardrobe, and wheelchair were made of wood scraps, toy wheels, etc. I refer to her paintings by creating a miniature scene-within-a-scene, as they appear in the minute reproductions. For example, the chair with scissors refers to Self-Portrait with Cropped Hair (1940); the constructed easel and wheelchair refer to the self-portrait on the easel.

JNANESHWAR'S DREAM, 2000.
12½ x 15½ x 11 inches.
*The source of illumination is
natural light filtered through
blue acetate mounted in the
ceiling, which bathes the room
in a dreamy hue.*

the motif, which is Kahlo's art. Bright colors can express whimsy and humor—but be careful not to overdo it, or use too many colors. Often a simple palette is stronger and more effective.

Choice of color is one of several elements that should serve the entire effect you seek. In *Van Gogh* (page 66), my aim was to mimic a painting of the artist's bedroom in Arles. While I had seen a reproduction of a version with subtler colors, I decided to use lilac for my work instead. I thought I was taking liberties, but when I finally saw another version of the Van Gogh painting, I was surprised to see it was the color I'd chosen.

In experiments with monochromatic schemes, I conceived of *Jnaneshwar's*

Dream for an exhibition titled "All Blues," which was how I rendered the room and its contents—everything blue: table grapes, clothes in the wardrobe, statue of Krishna, starry sky, the mirror reflection, and everything else. The inspiration for this work came from a devotional poem by the 13th-century Indian saint Jnaneshwar, who writes about his ubiquitous mystical vision of blueness: "The entire universe seems to be evenly manifested in blue," he sings, and "whatever I see [is] with a mind filled with this bluish hue." A copy of that wondrous poem lies in the trundle bed, on a blue quilt made from a waffle-weave scrap of a thermal undershirt. Another monochrome is a three-dimensional version of Matisse's painting *Red*

Studio (below). Here again I contradicted the rule about diminishing color: this is, after all, art about art! In fact, I replaced Matisse's brownish red with a brighter red in the miniature.

Just as costume and set designers use color to express character and milieu, I used color as emotional pointers for the set inspired by Mozart's opera *Don Giovanni*. In *Lecherous Appetites: The Banquet Scene* (right), I expressed manic, destructive egotism with a scheme of burgundy and silver: the dark red of blood or wine represents murder and lust, and the silver intimates cold amorality. In the banquet table, the scene's focal point, both colors are diminished to their palest versions—burgundy to pink and silver to white.

Color can be used both realistically and symbolically. *Hong Kong/Miami* (page 84) is a predominantly red box with tropical hues that express the harmony between

the exotic natures of two very different cities. The bright yellow and gold colors of *Sarastro's Sun* (page 3) are meant to express enlightenment, compassion, and spiritual love. In some back-and-front pieces, I employed both principles: one side modulated realistically, and in the other, throwing out the rules, creating a contrast between sobriety and whimsy.

LECHEROUS APPETITES: THE BANQUET SCENE, 2000. 18½ x 25½ x 18 inches. *The tablecloth becomes a bedsheet trailing off into a mass of boudoir pillows; the banquet table doubles as a bed of seduction Thus, the table turns into a double entendre of gluttony and lust. The life-size chandelier unifies the details. In the foreground is the set-up for Don Giovanni's private orchestra, including the score for* The Marriage of Figaro.

MATISSE, 1993. 11 x 14½ x 10½ inches. *The inspiration for this box was Matisse's* The Red Studio. *The furniture is either scratch-made or altered dollhouse items. For example, the grandfather clock is a dollhouse piece turned upside-down and backwards to eliminate detail and intensify the abstraction. The sculptures are made from modeling clay and Fimo. The pictures are my own renditions, or illustrations from magazines and postcards.*

COMPOSITION

A miniature is by definition a scene of compression, often with a lot of visual information packed into a small space. An analogous literary form that demonstrates compression is the Japanese haiku. In a famous 17th-century poem by Basho, three short lines render a sharp glimpse of a complete microcosmic event:

> Aged pond—
> Frog hops in—
> Kerplop!
>
> —*translation by Ichiro Kurihara*

Here a scene, a character, and an action unite in a sound-surprise (Kerplop!), which grants the reader (the poet's co-witness) a climactic moment of acute awareness.

UNTITLED, from "Modern Romance" series, David Levinthal, 1985. Polaroid sx-70 print, 3⅛ x 3⅛ inches. Courtesy Paul Morris Gallery, New York.

The miniature is an apt genre with which to compress such poignant, visual revelations. One way spatial compression can be achieved is through intimation, as in David Levinthal's coy, nocturnal vignettes, where narrative data is elided into psychological suggestiveness (below). Levinthal, a photographer, uses miniature props to brew mysterious, voyeuristic scenes conveying fleeting "instamatic" glimpses of life, as though seen through a train window or through the windshield of a passing car. By means of viewpoints that simultaneously evade and accentuate, Levinthal gives just enough information to communicate the enigmatic gist of a situation: an unknown woman takes leave of a movie theater; a car pulls into or away from an unidentified street corner. The photographs of these tabletop theaters suggest shadowy, impromptu moments; their allusive restraint allows the viewer to fill in the gaps with his own fantasies and dreams, as informed by his own psychological bent.

The photorealists exploit compression in a different way, through the technique of forced perspective. One clear example is Susan Leopold's *Under the Expressway* (opposite, top), which demonstrates the illusion of distance. The closest car is eight inches long, while the farther car, a Matchbox® toy, is about 1½ inches. They are in reality only a few inches apart, but appear to be very distant from each other. Leopold's compositions grant a certain leeway to the viewer, who optically travels like a movie-camera through a room or landscape. The observer can select his own vantage point, within limits, thus effectively changing the entire "picture." In this way, the viewer contributes to the piece as an active participant, choosing his angles and becoming a co-creator of the scene.

Like Leopold, John Mackiewicz uses variations of scale to suggest depth in his compositions. Perspective is compressed and distorted—essentially invented—to augment the drama and verisimilitude of his dioramas. Mackiewicz says, "The basic straight-on view of a piece has to be compositionally pleasing, just like a two-dimensional work of art." He advises against creating planes parallel or perpendicular to the viewer's point of view, instead suggesting swiveling the angle of the entire scene inside a box. "Canting" the scene will make one corner deep, which will maximize the pitch and create a more dynamic composition.

Alan Wolfson uses forced perspective to suggest a continuum of space. Peeking around corners, nooks, and crannies to glimpse rooms-beyond-rooms is a favorite Wolfson device. In *Non-stop Action* (below), we peep through a second-story window

UNDER THE EXPRESSWAY, Susan Leopold, 1988. Lens-Box mixed-media construction, 15½ x 16½ x 13½ inches. Courtesy of Jean Albano Gallery, Chicago, Illinois. *A sensational example of forced perspective using shifting scale. In a depth of only 13½ inches, Leopold has grouped Matchbox® and larger-size cars to create the illusion of distance.*

NON-STOP ACTION, Alan Wolfson, 1990. 14½ x 18 x 17 inches. Courtesy Louis K. Meisel Gallery, New York. *This half-inch-scale adult shop was based on a Times Square establishment, but the scene is a composite of many places.*

THE BAR AT THE STATION, John Mackiewicz, 1990. 12 x 18 x 14 inches. Courtesy O.K. Harris Works of Art, New York. *The book on the pile of suitcases is* Gulliver's Travels. *Outside the gate is an o-scale (1:48; a standard model rail- road scale where a foot is equal to 48 inches) passenger train. Behind that is an HO scale (1:87) car. Using forced perspec- tive, Mackiewicz created the illusion of distance.*

into someone's room, then through the door out to the hallway, then into yet another room across the hall. These compositional complexities are "rehearsed" by means of cardboard mock-ups that help approximate the sight lines, which determine how much detail will be visible, as well as the fit of the components.

Once the "stage" is planned, Wolfson relies on intuition to develop details, moving items around until he happens upon the most engaging arrangement. He also bases his designs on empirical observation: for example, if he himself were at the typewriter, where would he likely put down his coffee mug?

Next time you go to a theater, observe the stage sets to see how perspective is exaggerated. When you sit in a room, notice that the joins and planes of the walls appear to flare and bend. Because of perspective, lines appear to splay away from your vantage point, a paradox demonstrating the greater realism of illu- sion over fact.

As you begin composing a scene, keep your theme or intention in mind. What feeling or idea do you wish to convey? Then, as you proceed, allow the momentum of creativity to spontaneously unfold and guide you, for the creative process does have a life of its own.

USING YOUR SENSES

Why not engage the other senses, in addition to sight? Here are a few ideas to add scent, sound, and touch to a miniature scene.

• *Scent:* Place potpourri, loose aromatic tea, or cedar chips in miniaure bowls, or use as landscaping elements.

• *Sound:* Make miniature wind chimes from tiny shells, bits of metal and glass, and miniature bells. Add a miniature working clock for its ticking sounds (below).

• *Touch:* Texture is perceived not only through the hands—the eyes also register the roughness of brick, the smoothness of wood, the hardness of metal, and so on. Use a lively combination of materials to create intriguing textural designs.

DETAILS

If you use a working watch in your miniature, your roombox will become an actual timepiece. Mask the winding stem with the circular plastic collar from a bottle cap, or with any other snug-fitting circle or O-ring. To make a realistic looking, nonworking clock: Cut out watch ads from magazines. Select a frontal face with clear numbers. Laminate with laminating sheets or acetate from a stationery store, or with a bit of clear packing tape. Add three-dimensional "hands" made from toothpick ends, slivers of metal, pencil leads, or comb teeth. (Glue them on top of the existing hands in the picture.) Frame the clock in the collar of a bottle top, or in any circular metal or plastic shape. Or paste the clock face onto a metal-edged round key-tag.

LOST IN TIME, 1995. 16 X 14 X 9½ inches. Private collection. *A timepiece about clocks, made for a doctor who makes and collects them. Many of the miniature instruments work, and contribute ticking sounds and clockwork movements to the piece. I designed the box, which was built by a carpenter.*

MASS AND MESS

I once had a drawing teacher who advised us not to "torture the page." He said it so many times I thought he shouldn't torture us, either—but his point was well taken. Similarly, we shouldn't torture the viewer's eye. If you crowd your scenes with many elements, as I tend to do, it's best to arrange them in visual units, which are themselves arranged to suit the scene's overall composition.

Whether your scene is congested or spare, the arrangement of things should allow the viewer to "read" it. If you want to clutter a tabletop (see Wolfson's *Times Square Hotel Room*, left), group small details together, leaving some space for the surface to "breathe" and for the eye to take it all in. Negative space, the equivalent of silence in music, is as important as positive space. *Gizmos* (page 43) appears to be an all-over abstraction, yet there's an organizing rhythm to the congestion. In the same way, despite the excessive details of *Cloak and Candles* (above), the eye is kept from getting lost because of focal points amid the clutter.

STASIS AND MOVEMENT

Space is invigorated by diagonals, asymmetry, and by moving the focus away from the center of the composition. When the center is the focus, one of two things happens: the composition seems stuck, or it appears still. In the middle of Grand Central Station in New York is an information kiosk with a big clock. If you wanted to find someone amid the thousands of rushing commuters, you'd probably tell your friend to meet you "under the clock." Like the eye of a storm, all the frenetic, random activity halts at this hub.

A composition can be deliberately centered to invoke a desirable stillness. Altars and shrines, which are often symmetrical, convey qualities of serenity, strength, and stability. The viewer does not come to a sudden halt, but rather is drawn into the vortex of inner stillness. The jewel-like, filigree palaces of Barbara Minch (page 24) have this effect, as do some of the highbrow, serene assemblages of Rosemary Butler (page 73). In *The Queen of the Night* (page 121), I placed the tower stage-center to indicate the fixated madness and impenetrability of the Queen.

A tableau is less artificially static and more visually stimulating when animated through uneven arrangements. For example, in *The Papermaker's Studio* (above, right), Diane Price maneuvers the objects in such a way as to relieve the rectangularity of the enclosure. For interesting combinations of stasis and movement, study Old Master paintings. In the background of the canvas there might be a

building, the frame of a window, a mountain range. The action occurs in the foreground—a battle is fought, a group of peasants are dancing, a hunt thunders by.

The miniaturist can infuse a still scene with the suggestion of activity in countless ways. A shade-cord bending into a room suggests a breeze (see *Edward Hopper*, page 67). A bed or bureau pulled slightly away from the wall will instantly activate a stagnant room. Skew the rug or lay its design on the diagonal. Well-placed interruptions agitate space, so you might consider interjecting a structural column that will link floor to ceiling and churn up the space (below). The placement of

Above:
THE PAPERMAKER'S STUDIO, Diane Price, 1993. 9 x 5¼ x 6 inches. *The angled position of a few objects relieves the static nature of the box. The "primitive" box is in keeping with the usual gritty nature of an artist's workspace.*

Left:
Detail of structural column, HIDING PLACES, 1996.

FRIDAY NIGHT RERUN, Susan
Leopold, 1986. Lens-Box
mixed-media construction,
11¼ x 8½ x 8 inches.
Courtesy of Jean Albano
Gallery, Chicago, Illinois.
*Leopold explains: ". . . Doors
lead off to undefined territories,
mirrors provide vistas into
spaces not visible from a particular vantage point, windows
reveal voyeuristic moments into
other interiors . . . a corner is
no longer an entrapment but a
space beyond."*

furniture need not be entirely rational—
but it must work compositionally. Aim for
a slight uneasiness by adding a judicious
touch of dissonance; you'll leave something for the viewer to work out.

Even if you wish to convey stately
formality, you don't have to resort to predictable and monotonous arrangements.
Say you create a formal dining room
dominated by symmetry: a central fireplace flanked by twin armoires, a table
with six identical settings and three candlesticks at each end. It's perfect. In fact, it's
too perfect. It doesn't breathe, and lacks
both compositional and narrative interest.
Nudge the angle of a chair slightly so that
it will seem recently occupied. Disturb the
place settings a bit, regroup the candles
asymmetrically in uneven tiers, and vary
their lengths. Allow some element to jut
or angle disobediently into the room: a
book forgotten on a chair, half hidden
beneath the hem of the tablecloth. Stand

one of the armoires in front of a panel or
pilaster, jockeyed slightly in front of its
twin. The trick is to permeate formality
subtly with the informal, human appeal
of the irregular.

Arrangements should never become
formulaic. Take the case of a bedroom
that's so orderly, your response is to want
to crawl into the unrumpled bed for a
little nap. If tedium is your intention, or
if you're after an antidote for insomnia,
then don't move a thing. But if you want
to stimulate the viewer, then create a little
disturbance. Leave the jewelry box open,
provokingly accessible. Throw a blanket
obliquely over the bed, with a corner
trailing irresponsibly on the floor. Leave
drawers open to suggest some kind of
animate presence. And of course, there's
the psychological intrigue of apertures. A
door that's closed is just closed. But a
door that's cracked open—you can't help
but wonder what lies beyond.

VISUAL RHYME
AND ASSONANCE

The rhyming of shapes through the repetition of forms is a fundamental element of visual art that unifies and strengthens a composition. Just as we love rhymes in songs, we appreciate repeated shapes in visual contexts. Years ago I heard a lecture at the Barnes Foundation, in Merion, Pennsylvania, which houses an extraordinary collection of European paintings. We were being taught to analyze the abstract elements of a certain Old Master portrait of an old man. What made the painting so strong? We were asked to look beyond the narrative nobility registered in the beautifully painted face, and regard only the composition. "Look at the man's ear," the lecturer hinted, "do you see ears anywhere else on the canvas?" Suddenly I could see "ears" all over the painting—in the swirls of his clothes, in the painterly brushwork of the background—all of which subtly built up the painting into a powerful unity. The "rhyme-scheme" of the ear-shape in varied repetition contributed to the greatness of that painting.

In miniatures, we can use the same principle of compositional unity. Does the shape of one thing remind you of the shape of something else? By abstracting the essence of objects we can discern that a rose, vase, wineglass, and table are fundamentally a circle, rectangle, triangle, and square. In Rosemary Butler's assemblage *'Tis Edna Ferber's Fate* (above),

which contains Ferber's book with the ironic title *So Big*, the basic design shape is the oval. The ovals of the shoes set the design's main shape, which is echoed in the oval lid of the antique box, the oval mirror, and the oval line of the pearl necklace.

'TIS EDNA FERBER'S FATE, Rosemary Butler, undated. Wood, paper, glass, leather, faux pearls, and lace in a wood box, 22½ x 17½ x 4 inches.

FORTRESS, 1992. 24 x 32 x 15¼ inches. *This imaginary underground orphanage is built inside an armature of chicken wire and papier-mâché. The curve of the hubcap which suggests refuge, is echoed throughout, all the way down to the curvy toy dragon. The blankets are pieces of the reverse side of faded flannel shirts. The headboards are hinges, metal plates, drawer pulls, and other hardware.*

In *Fortress* (above), I used recurring curves for the theme of refuge and for formal unity. Arches appear throughout—in the hubcap, the plate rim, the shaped papier-mâché walls. The shape is echoed down to the smallest details, from headboards to toys, even to the humps in the dragon's back. In *Sarastro's Egyptian Room* (opposite, bottom), triangles support the formal and symbolic theme of the pyramid. We read the interior as pyramidal because of three dominant triangular elements arranged into a larger triangle composed of the steel pyramid, the dollar-bill pyramid, and the bust on its stand.

The literary device of assonance, or inexact rhyme, has a counterpart in visual art. In *The Steamship* (opposite, top), the boat in the picture echoes the shape of the chair back, and the steam curves similarly to the wallpaper pattern. Why use assonance instead of perfect rhyme? While the repetition of shapes supports its composition, identical elements can be tedious. Experiment by altering exact duplications into approximate rhyme instead. For instance, two matching trees might work better if you made one of them a column. You can modify elements by changing material, shape, and size, or by breaking

up redundant verticality through random branching. As you work with shapes, whether in two or three dimensions, you'll develop an eye for rhyme and off-rhyme, and begin intuitively to choose elements that strengthen your art.

THE STEAMSHIP, 1996. 10 x 13 x 9 inches. *The television is a metal pencil sharpener with the image on the screen painted out. The wallpapers are from decorative boxes; the curve-patterned wall is a book cover. The ceiling fixture is a button; the window is broken Plexi.*

Detail, SARASTRO'S EGYPTIAN ROOM (TEMPLE OF DENDUR) from THE MAGIC FLUTE series, 1997–99. 20 x 18 x 18 inches. *The steel pyramid at the left is the cut-out hoist-hole from a steel plank used in the street to cover a construction-pit.*

ON A SCALE OF
ONE TO TWELVE

GREENWICH VILLAGE COFFEE HOUSE, 1992. 12 X 25 X 20 inches. Private collection. *This replica of a typical Greenwich Village bistro incorporates cake supports, a hose connector, a wine rack, a watch, mahjong tiles, finials, mirrors, and other common objects. Each table reveals a little story about its unseen occupant.*

Scale is the comparative measurement of different elements within a system. We take scale for granted until an anomaly occurs. If you enter a room that has a six-foot pencil propped against the wall, you might be taken aback. There's an anecdote about a now famous painter from the Midwest who came to New York as a young man to paint billboards. He arrived at night, checked into the YMCA, and saw nothing of the city until the next morning, when he poked his head out the door and had his first glimpse of the Empire State Building. Pulling back in shock, he exclaimed: "Whoa, I better get me another cup of coffee before I go out there!" He'd probably never seen anything taller than a silo! Ironically, his job had him painting faces five feet tall and smiles a yard wide.

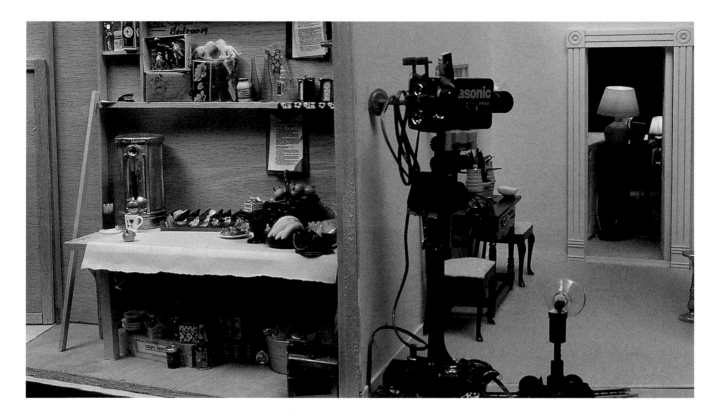

The twist in an old *Twilight Zone* episode has to do with scale. A solitary old woman lives in an isolated cabin that a tiny alien spacecraft invades one night. We identify with her fear and helplessness; our sympathy and concern are engaged as the rocketship torments her like a stinging wasp. In the last scene, the camera zooms in on the wing of the craft. We see an emblem: USA. In a shocking perceptual switch, we realize that the pilots are human, which means that she is not! She is, in fact, an extraterrestrial colossus!

DELIBERATE DEVIATION

Standard dollhouse scale, one inch to a foot, is popular among artists because building components in that scale are so available. While one-inch scale is convenient, it's best not to depend solely on it. Consciously deviating from uniform or predictable scale will enliven most any scene. Eric Edelman mixes scale within the four partitions of his *Hommage à Joseph, René, et Robert* (page 64) to great effect. Experiment, surprise your eyes—don't be afraid to break rules of logic.

To mix scales, you might include real-life objects with miniatures. I've seen the work of a European miniaturist who juxtaposes vintage plumbing fixtures with one-inch scale furniture in his magical and poetic boxed scenes. In *Greenwich Village Coffee House* (opposite), the rafter comes from a wine rack; *Superior Banister* (page 62) incorporates a section of a real stair banister; and *Secret Zone* (page 63) rests on part of a traffic barricade. *Cloak and Candles* (page 54) incorporates a chair leg as a fluted column.

Detail, CRAFT SERVICES, TELEVISION STUDIO, 1991. A 360-degree diorama, 32 x 34 x 14 inches. *An example of adapting real-life objects into a miniature scene: The cameras are batteries, the lights are suction cups, and the dolly tracks (visible at the very bottom of the photo) are from a model railroad. The coffee tureen is a plumbing connector.*

SUPERIOR BANISTER, 1994.
12 x 9 x 5 inches. *A small
section of a stair banister serves
as the parapet to a miniature
warehouse.*

Mixing scales is a way to achieve
forced perspective, as in Susan Leopold's
Under the Expressway (page 51). Leopold's
camera-obscura-like vignettes demonstrate
how diverse scales enhance the drama and
realism of a scene. The viewer peers
through the distortion of a fish-eye lens
at a lifelike yet off-balanced image, and is
treated to a bout of vertigo, a voyeuristic
shock, or a sudden psychological plunge.

Sometimes deviations in scale can
have symbolic as well as visual significance.
In addition to being a play on scale, the
chairs in Charles Mingus III's *Underground
World* (opposite, top) have a sociological
connotation. This piece represents a hole
in the ground, symbolic of economic
life below the poverty line. The chair is a
metaphor for ownership; its scale represents a lack of sufficiency and destitution.

Likewise, the adaptation of real-life items into miniature scenes can at times be tongue-in-cheek, with objects meant to appear true-to-scale to accentuate their lilliputian surroundings. In the attic of the MacKenzie-Childs *Miniature Mansion*, the Mouse House is furnished with human-scale objects, which the mice seem to have appropriated for their own use. The conservatory boasts tiny, live birds, and an aquarium is stocked with diminutive living fish, in fractal-like replications of ordinary or expected scale.

However, despite the benefits of deliberate deviation, scale that's accidentally off can spoil the effect you're seeking. For example, a too-thick rug could form overly large buckling, which would detract from a scene. Furniture made from wood that is too thick looks clunky and oppressive; if the wood is too thin, the furniture appears flimsy and implausible.

"UNDERGROUND WORLD," or "BILL BRADLEY ECONOMICS CHART #1," Charles Mingus III, undated. Dirt, handmade chairs, and mirrors in an illuminated, hinged glass-framed box. Inside dimensions: 4¾ x 11½ x 17½ inches. *This piece is about economics, scale, and numbers. The chairs are metaphors of ownership. On the wall, a flickering panel displays a UFO—a way out of the hole.*

SECRET ZONE, 1992, 18½ x 19¼ x 7 inches. Private collection. *The base of this assemblage is a fragment from a street barricade.*

PLANNING AND IMPROVISATION

Below:
Detail, HOMMAGE À JOSEPH,
RENÉ, ET ROBERT, Eric
Edelman, 1996–2000.
10 X 15½ X 10½. Photo © 2001
Aaron Norman. *In this piece,
Edelman wished "to revisit
Cornell and Magritte themes
in an atmosphere of humor,
wonder, and gentle irony."*

Right:
Edelman's Hommage *seen
from above.*

In any of the visual arts, there's often a balance between planning and improvisation. In Eric Edelman's *Hommage à Joseph, Rene, et Robert,* a box-sculpture tribute to the artist's most important influences, Joseph Cornell and René Magritte, only the main "room" was planned; the three smaller sections evolved as the work progressed. Edelman says: "My boxes have always been ordered improvisations of found objects. As I work, I

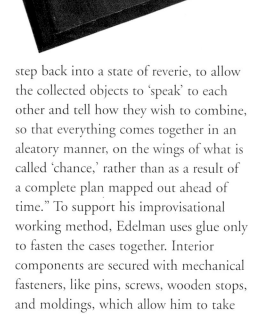

step back into a state of reverie, to allow the collected objects to 'speak' to each other and tell how they wish to combine, so that everything comes together in an aleatory manner, on the wings of what is called 'chance,' rather than as a result of a complete plan mapped out ahead of time." To support his improvisational working method, Edelman uses glue only to fasten the cases together. Interior components are secured with mechanical fasteners, like pins, screws, wooden stops, and moldings, which allow him to take apart and reassemble a tableau as often as desired.

To put it another way, if intention is like an anchor, the boat—your art—should be allowed to drift in the currents of creative impetus. In my experience, it's that "drift" that gives the work its lively freshness. The boat should engage with the water and dance with the wind—not become landlocked, or stuck in dry-dock, as with rigid control and overplanning.

THEMES AND VARIATIONS

There are countless themes available to miniaturists, with subjects that can be rendered in any styles as vast tableaux, minute still-lifes, or anything between. They can be abstract, representative, or a combination of the two. Among other approaches, miniatures can be conceived as homages, made to honor other works of art or artists. Miniatures can also be narratives, designed to represent a story or event.

HOMAGES

Artists have always made homages to their predecessors, and the miniature is a perfect genre for extending this tradition. An exquisite example is Edelman's *Hommage* (opposite). In the main "room" of this complex box is a three-dimensional version of Magritte's *La durée poignardée (Time Transfixed)* (The Art Institute of Chicago), a painting used by Cornell in a memorial collage to honor his brother Robert, a model-train enthusiast. At the rear of the box, viewed from above, are three smaller partitions that contain references to the works of Cornell and Magritte: pipes, mirrors, drinking glasses, the color blue, the heavens, multiples of objects, and the written word. The central room contains a tiny scene evoking Cornell's *Pink Palace* series of constructions (page 13). This piece was the first Cornell work that Edelman ever saw.

Rosemary Butler has created an homage to Picasso in her *Still Life with*

THE NICE PIANO LESSON *or* MY METAMORPHOSED MATISSE, Rosemary Butler, undated. Wood, paper, glass, leather, faux pearls, lace in wood box, lighted indirectly by a 4-watt bulb, 22½ x 17½ x 4 inches.

Cane Table (page 73), and an homage to Matisse (above). *The Nice Piano Lesson* or *My Metamorphosed Matisse* is a three-dimensional interpretation of Matisse's painting *The Piano Lesson* (Museum of Modern Art, New York). In Butler's work, all of the elements of the Matisse are switched: Paris has been turned into the South of France; the French boy student has become an American Victorian girl who is flanked not by two females, as in

VAN GOGH, 1991. 10 X 13½ X 11½ inches. *This is the first of a series of boxes based on great paintings, in which I restored the third dimension that the artist eliminated. Everything is handmade except for the table and the doors, which are doll-house items. The chairs were made from kits. I added elements from other Van Gogh paintings: a sunflower, pipe, and tobacco.*

the Matisse, but by Van Cliburn and Orpheus. Matisse's gray/green garden has been transformed into a sea and sky of blues and black representing day and night. Butler puns with the word "Nice." She also contrives an elaborate rebus composed of a compass pointing North, underneath blocks of ice (N + ice). This is a great example of how one can use emulation as a springboard for original work.

For other homages to art, see *Matisse* (page 49), *Van Gogh* (below), *Florine Stettheimer* (page 44), *Rousseau* (opposite, top), *Hopper* (opposite, bottom), *Vuillard* (page 79), and *Frida Kahlo* (page 47), as well as John Mackiewicz's *Room with a*

View (page 46), which was inspired by a painting by Edward Hopper.

NARRATIVES

Miniaturists are especially susceptible to storytelling, whether their locales are based on reality, as in David Malcolm Rose's work; imagination, as in Rosemary Butler's; or a combination of both, like Alan Wolfson's. To a large extent Wolfson modifies actual places to make the composition a work of art, insisting that design always takes precedence over fidelity to fact. His intense narratives are built up

ROUSSEAU, 1996. 12 X 17 X 11 inches. *This scene, based on the painting* The Dream *(Museum of Modern Art, New York), omits Rousseau's reclining nude. The couch was made from inch-scale tabletops and "upholstered" in red velvet. The flowers are antique enamel pins.*

EDWARD HOPPER, 1996. 16 X 17 X 17 inches. Private collection. *This box is an homage to Hopper's* Office at Night *(Walker Art Center, Minneapolis, Minnesota), without figures. Except for the chairs, the furniture and woodwork are handmade.*

LION OIL, David Malcolm Rose, 1990. 16 x 36 x 34 inches. Collection of Janette and Charles Heinbockle. *David Rose's work documents the end of an era, before the super highways replaced individually-owned businesses with huge chain stores. The Lion Oil stood just south of Little Rock, Arkansas, along the old Pine Bluff highway. Its name is a palindrome.*

and supported by accumulations of anecdotal details that form a kind of reticent story line. As you look at his dioramas, you might catch yourself telling a story. For example: Out the window of the sad and seedy *Times Square Hotel Room* (page 54) flash the lights of New York's red-light district. Inside, details help piece together a profile of the unseen occupant, from the shaving cream in the medicine chest and the pinup on the wall, to the exposed plumbing and empty toilet paper rolls left on the bathroom floor. On the sill, the binoculars, radio (with antenna aimed perhaps significantly at the street), and overflowing ashtray reveal that the tenant habitually sits looking out the window. The presence of a typewriter is open to interpretation. Is he a writer? We'll never know his name, but we gather his story from the clues Wolfson submits.

Narrative is crucial to every inch of a Wolfson diorama. In *Miss America Diner* (page 36), even the diner's rooftop is utilized to enact the drama of an air

conditioner being overhauled. Our eyes report the story: our gaze climbs the ladder to the roof, which now becomes a stage. The inspection plate has been removed from the air conditioner and tools are everywhere. The old fan motor is out of its casing, and a new one is waiting to be installed. And when we enter the interior of the diner, we encounter a scene *in medias res*. On the tables are little tales of unfinished meals. Through the side windows, over the phones, we see into the lavatory, and a partially open door admits us to a storeroom full of fast-food staples.

As another photorealist, David Malcolm Rose says: "I guess I'm a story-teller. I tell stories about the 'Lost Highways'—the end of an era of regional diversity." Each of Rose's tableaux is the portrait of a building, an era, and a population of service concessionaires and consumers—the highway travelers of America. The buildings are about their human occupants, who lived above or behind the motels, filling stations, diners, and general stores they ran. In the office of *Lion Oil* (opposite), there are still papers in the drawers of the battered office desk. In *Joubert's* (below), Rose speculates that as Mr. Joubert's business began to slacken, he took to staying upstairs until a customer called. He'd have a second cup of coffee and wait. If you were to rattle the door and yell up, Rose says, he may come down even now. *The Satellite* (page 19), a 1950s roadside eatery, carries the vivid visual events that makes for a good story too.

The narrative imagination of John Mackiewicz is evident throughout his dioramas. He feels that these composites of fleeting impressions are a reliable method with which to capture the aura of generic situations. Mackiewicz's research is memory, both in visual data and emotional associations that serve to distill the essence of an environment. His work is informed by his own experience, as well as by painting and film. The appeal and power of the work comes from this distil-

lation of stark, matter-of-fact reality. The observers of his narratives, no matter where they come from, have also experienced these nether realms; their startling yet subliminal impact evokes a sense of *déjà vu*, exposing themes that might make us recoil in recognition, as they strike places within us that many might prefer to keep under wraps.

JUKE JOINT, John Mackiewicz, 1991. 12 x 14 x 12 inches. Courtesy O.K. Harris Works of Art, New York. *Juke joints are generally found on highways in the southern portion of the United States. Outside the window, Mackiewicz wanted to indicate the presence of street and automobile lights to contrast the interior dimness. The chrome details on the jukebox come from 1950s model cars, as jukeboxes of that era were designed to resemble Chevys and other cars, complete with fins and grilles.*

JOUBERT'S, David Malcolm Rose, 1991. 15 x 18 x 21 inches. Collection of the artist. *David Rose creates portraits of roadside lives. The artist came upon this building on his travels in Louisiana.*

USING FIGURES

Detail, BACK STREET, John Mackiewicz, 1991. 12 x 18 x 14 inches. Courtesy O.K. Harris Works of Art, New York. *Mackiewicz feels that human figures would detract from the realism of the art. The female mannequin is a composite of four dolls. The cobblestone street was made from spackling putty, scored to look like paving stones. The beer ad is a working neon sign.*

Everyone seems to have a strong opinion about including human or animal figures in a miniature scene. I don't use representatives of living creatures for two main reasons: they always seem implausible, and it's been my experience that keeping the scene uninhabited allows the viewer imaginatively to slip inside. The presence of a "person" subverts the subliminal invitation for the viewer to venture in, and with no psychological room or reason to enter, the viewer tends to linger on the sidelines.

Many artists concur. The arresting spaces Susan Leopold creates are devoid of people, yet suggest that something has happened or is about to. This is true in the work of David Rose, John Mackiewicz, and Alan Wolfson, who imply human occupation through emblems: papers forgotten in an office desk drawer, a beer left on a bathroom sink, a television flickering in a rented room. Wolfson says that seeing miniature graffiti and garbage is more believable than seeing a miniature person.

Similarly, Mackiewicz maintains that the artifacts of human presence evoke more intensity and feeling than dolls can. In *Back Street* (opposite), Mackiewicz parodies the use of figures in miniatures with the armless dummy in the window, maintaining that "It is impossible to reproduce the plasticity of human skin or the natural animation of the human form in miniature." Yet, his desolate rooms are filled with presence. That folding chair in *Juke Joint* (page 69) will remain curiously empty. But as I look at it, I come to the disquieting awareness that *I* am sitting there. And I'm left startled and amused, yet oddly gratified, caught in this ironic psychological trap.

Some artists do incorporate figures in ways that do not detract from the strength or credibility of a work. Rosemary Butler, with elegant, sparing deliberation, incorporates figurines in her metaphorical scenes, which read not as stand-ins for "people" but as objects no more animate than the piano, wine glass, and high chair (page 65).

I know of only one successful use of figures in miniature art, which is in the work of David Levinthal (above). Levinthal's tour de force depends on the fact that his medium ultimately is photography, by way of miniature tableaux. Yet because he is interested less in literal depiction than in the power of suggestion, the scenes at their three-dimensional stage probably would be as startlingly "real" as are the ethereal realness of the photos. Levinthal's technical and artistic talent,

UNTITLED, from "Modern Romance" series, David Levinthal, 1985. Polaroid sx-70 print, 3⅛ x 3⅛ inches. Courtesy Paul Morris Gallery, New York.

Above and right:
GRAMERCY PARK, 1994.
12 x 12 x 10 inches.

especially with composition and lighting, renders the figures in these suggestive nocturnes real not in the sense of photo-realism, but because of their persuasive-ness, universality, and ability to evoke a heightened response of strange familiarity.

Having said that, you might be wondering what those three golden retrievers are doing in my diorama of Gramercy Park (above). I wouldn't have included them, except that this was a wedding-gift commission from a bride to her groom, and the animals were requisite to the scene she had in mind. Compare the picture with the golden retrievers to the detail shot that omits the dogs (left). Which do you think works better? Of course, whether or not you include figures, and how, will be a decision you'll make for yourself.

VISUAL PUNNING

"SLIGHT" OF HAND

A pun can work visually as well as verbally, when an object signifies something in addition to what it denotes. Rosemary Butler uses "wrought irony" in much of her work, as when she plays with "cane" in her *Still Life with Cane Table* (right).

A more sedate example of visual punning is the medieval *Crib of the Infant Jesus*, in the Metropolitan Museum of Art, New York. The sides of this doll-size bed are decorated with shapes resembling vaulted church windows, a double meaning that signifies, perhaps, the birth of Jesus as the birth of the Church.

In *The Flying Machine* (below, right), from the *Magic Flute* opera series, the bridge cables become a conceptual pun: the piano strings from which they were made also look like the staves on sheet music. In stage productions, the "flying machine" used by the three spirit-guides is often a movable cloud. Here, to extend the pun, the flying machine is New York City's Roosevelt Island tram, a real "flying machine." Roosevelt is Dutch for "World of Roses," and roses, the Masonic symbol of purity, and emblems for the three spirit-guides.

The Queen of the Night (page 121), also from *The Magic Flute* series, was modeled after the Soldiers and Sailors Memorial on Riverside Drive, New York. The monument resembles the mountain out of which the Queen appears at the beginning of the opera. In Masonic symbolism, the Corinthian columns stand for

exuberance and action, qualities vocalized in the Queen's sparking arias. In the final act, *Sarastro's Sun* dominates the stage. For the miniature version, I created a replica of the sunburst chandelier in the Metropolitan Opera House (page 3). Both the miniature and the actual chandelier are made of Austrian crystal.

STILL LIFE WITH CANE TABLE, Rosemary Butler, undated. Wood, paper, clay, metal, plastic, and fiber in a wood box, 11¼ x 13 x 7½ inches. *Inspired by Picasso's* Still Life with Cane Chair, *a collage framed in rope, Butler framed her miniature table in rope. The objects in the Picasso are on her table, but Picasso's "JOUR" (Journal) has become "Her" (Herald) from the masthead of the* Miami Herald. *The plastic cane is a play on words.*

THE FLYING MACHINE (ROOSEVELT ISLAND TRAM) from THE MAGIC FLUTE series, 1997–99. 21 x 30 x 12 inches. *The bridge cables are piano strings. The monumental "M" stands for Mozart, Magic, Mason, Music—and Miniature!*

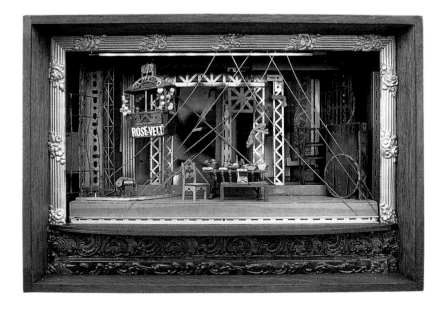

PART III
PASS THE GLUE

THINGS TO MAKE, AND MAKING THINGS

"Any area of human endeavor is open for interpretation in miniature."

—SYBIL HARP, Editor Emeritus, *Dollhouse Miniatures* magazine

Detail, FELISSIMO TOWNHOUSE. 1993, 50 x 30 x 19 inches (entire structure).

WALLS

Shy wallflowers don't get noticed, and
insipid wallpaper will make paltry
impact. There are many alternative wall
treatments to commercial dollhouse wallpaper. To guide you toward unexpected,
dynamic, and original solutions, here are
some ideas:

• Use your computer to make wallpaper patterns by printing out graphics
on colored paper. You can add more color
with felt-tip pens, colored pencils, or
rubber stamps.

• Consider using real-scale wallpaper
in a miniature scene. Cleverly mixing
scales can be dramatic and unexpected.

• Scumble the wall with layers of
waterbased hobby paints. To achieve a
two-tone look, first paint the wall with
the bottom color. When dry, use a sponge
to lightly dapple on a lighter shade or a
contrasting color. (This was how the
interior walls for *Felissimo* were done.)

• Paint or stencil friezes close to the
ceiling. One way to make stencils is with

THE MUD ROOM from THE MINIATURE MANSION, MacKenzie-Childs, 1998. *A room in the Miniature Mansion for flower-drying and plant-potting, and connected to the greenhouse. The wallpaper is newspaper, and the paintings are of animals. Equally creative, the master bedroom in the Miniature Mansion is diaper-patterned (see page 85).*

Detail, HIDING PLACES, 1996. *The left-hand wall is a found oil-on-masonite painting.*

card stock: simply punch designs with decorative hole punches (flowers, leaves, stars, etc.). You can also make friezes from a strip of decorative paper, such as origami, giftwrap, or dollhouse wallpaper. It's a nice touch to separate the paper frieze from the painted wall with half-round or chair-rail molding.

• To make walls of "limestone blocks" (interior or exterior), section the wall into a grid using the narrowest available graphics tape (in art supply stores). Then lightly sponge on limestone colors. If you want to simulate "veins," as in marble, use the sharp point of an eraser to pick up some of the pigment before it dries. To make speckles, flick thinned paint off of an old toothbrush. Remove the tape once the paint is dry.

• Simulate ornate plaster designs by squeezing plaster (or spackling compound) out of a pastry bag fitted with the finest nozzle. When dry, the designs can be painted to simulate gold or silver leaf. Some spackling compounds come in a squeezeable tube with a plastic tip. Snip the tip to whatever thickness of beading you desire.

• Use envelope privacy liners with delicate patterns. Trim the usable portions and collage directly onto the wall with spray-mount.

• Vary the texture of a wall by including wainscoting or other wood paneling (see detail, *Hiding Places,* page 80).

• Interrupt walls and ceilings with soffets, pipes, and other protrusions (see detail, *Hiding Places,* page 112). Other

Detail, FELISSIMO TOWN-
HOUSE, 1993, 50 x 30 x 19
inches (entire structure).
*I built curved walls in several
rooms of the Felissimo townhouse. The curve was achieved
by cutting a section from a
6"-diameter cardboard tube.*

DICHOTOMY, Diane Price,
1995. Mixed media, 17 x 11 x
5 inches. *You can decorate
walls with interesting giftwrap
or use handmade, textured
paper, as Diane Price does here.
Notice one side of the roombox
is angled to create a more
inviting space.*

solutions to enlivening a banal wall are
bookshelves (right), prominent utility
shelves, or abbreviated attics.

• Just about any material meant for
floors can be used on walls, including
carpeting. You can use pressed ceiling tin
(from dollhouse shops) on walls, or find
sheets of thin metal with small, embossed
patterns. You can use floor tiles, bricks,
and the like on walls, too. (See pages
80–82 for more ideas.)

• Large mirrors will expand and
duplicate space, and reflect hard-to-see
details. Because they are reflective, mirrors
are also a source of light.

OTHER DECORATIVE EFFECTS

Decorate paper to create your own unique wall coverings. Here are three easy techniques that will produce attractive patterns and textures:

1. *For a "cracked ice" effect:* Paint a sheet of good-quality watercolor paper with watercolor, ink, or thinned water-based hobby paint. The paper could be either hot-press (smooth) or cold-press (rough). While still wet, cover the paper with material like bubble wrap, crinkled aluminum foil, or wrinkled plastic wrap. Weight the covered paper with heavy books until the paint dries. Spray-mount the decorative paper to the wall, or use wallpaper glue, avoiding ripples and air pockets.

2. *For a similar crackled effect:* Spray one side of household plastic wrap with paint. Lay a sheet of paper on a flat surface, then press the plastic wrap, paint side down, onto the paper. Before the paint dries, you can mark patterns with the edge of a pencil eraser, or after it dries, you can add other colors from a spray bottle or by lightly sponging over the design.

3. *For a classic "resist" technique:* On a sheet of heavy paper, make a design with wax crayons or oil pastel sticks. Paint over the design with watercolors. The wax or oil will resist the paint, making fascinating patterns.

VUILLARD, 1992. 13½ x 24½ x 15¼ inches. *Another way to divide up and decorate spaces is by using folding screens, as illustrated in this homage to the artist Edvard Vuillard. The plastic screen, which I painted ebony, came from Chinatown, and originally held pictures of flowers, which I replaced with Origami patterns.*

FLOORS

The variety of floor treatments seems endless. You can cover a floor with narrow boards, wide planks, and geometric parquetry; with brick, stone, tile, and marble; with carpets, rugs, and mats; you can even simulate concrete or a glossy deck finish.

• Wooden plank floors are available commercially, but it's fun, easy, and more original to make your own. In *Van Gogh* (page 66), I cut each irregular plank out of strip-wood, painted them individually, and glued them to the floor. You can use pegs or nails in floorboards. For pegs, make a small hole with a nail or awl, insert a fragment of toothpick or tiny dowel, hammer it in, and sand it down. For nails, use miniature-scale nails and a small hammer.

• In *Mangia* (right), the "flagstone" floor was made by painting a piece of gray cardboard with various shades of brown, then cutting out random shapes and gluing them down like pieces in a puzzle.

• One-inch-square "marble" tiles are available from dollhouse stores in all the variegated colors of real marble. To simulate worn linoleum, I place them face-down with the gray backs showing.

• Plastic sheets of patterned "tile" are available in dollhouse stores. When using these prefabricated floors, I prefer to mix-and-match patterns for variety and originality. For a matte finish, lightly paint the sheet, then rub off the paint.

• Full-scale, one- or two-inch ceramic floor tiles translate into one- or two-foot tiles in a miniature room or patio.

• One-inch-scale terracotta bricks or square terracotta tiles can either be laid down individually in unique patterns, as I did for the patio in *Bungalow* (page 82); or as a unit (the bricks come on a mesh backing). I use ordinary spackling compound rather than dollhouse mortar for installing and grouting my tiles.

• Contact paper comes in a variety of marble, tile, and brick patterns that can be used for flooring in miniatures. If

Opposite:
Detail, HIDING PLACES, 1996.
An example of a linoleum floor. The floor runner is a piece of brocade ribbon. The TV antenna is a hairpin.

Entryway, MANGIA, 1995.
25 x 18 x 36 inches. Private collection.

RUGS

MIAMI BEACH BUNGALOW, 1995. 15 x 18 x 29 inches. Private collection. *The African sculpture is an authentic African figurine. The ovoid vase was a clear plastic egg. The furniture was made with Eric Edelman's help.*

UPTOWN LIVING ROOM, 1991. 12 x 36 x 36 inches (entire structure). *The back side of a bit of Naugahyde was used for the wall-to-wall carpeting. The round "glass" table top in the dining alcove is the lid of a yogurt container. The standing lamp was made of a watercolor brush and a suction cup.*

using brick-patterned paper, consider painting some of the bricks, or spraying the sheet with a mist of gray to mottle the uniform pattern.

• Try painting or stenciling designs on a floor. Look through interior design and decorating books and magazines for pattern ideas.

Area rugs and mats can be found in textile sample books, sewing supply and fabric stores, and hardware stores. In *Hiding Places* (page 80), the carpet runner is a length of brocade from a textile store (you could also use wire-edged ribbon). Make a welcome mat from a Velcro® square. Dot "Welcome" on the mat with a fine-tipped, permanent marker.

For the thick-pile rug in *Miami Beach Bungalow* (left), I used fluffy material from a fabric store. For the carpeting in *Hopper* (page 67), I used velvet from a fabric store (I made sure the scale of the pile was correct). An advantage of using real velvet is that you can simulate tread marks by roughing up the pile. I use the reverse, feltlike side of cheap vinyl upholstery material for short-pile, wall-to-wall carpets (see *Uptown Living Room*, below).

CEILINGS

I'm always on the lookout for new ways the ceiling can contribute interest to a room. In addition to lighting fixtures, you can enhance a ceiling with architectural layers. Here are some ideas:

• Use moldings to give weight and texture to a blank ceiling. Moldings and cornices can be bought at dollhouse stores, or built up with layers of wood trim. You can make dentil molding from small blocks cut from wood strips, or use Legos (see *Mangia*, right) and other building toys.

• Use one or more wooden plaques, painted or stained if desired, to make a "dropped" ceiling or "plaster" medallion (see "Medallions," page 85). Or use small, fancy picture frames to make a "raised" ceiling. (Remove the glass, mat, and backing, then paint or stain the frame before gluing it to the ceiling.) Consider using the back side of the frame, which may be more visually interesting than the front.

• Horizontal beams are a good means of activating a ceiling. The beams can be rough-hewn or even, and can contrast with or match the ceiling color. Corbels from miniatures shops can be used to support beams, or they can be arranged in facing pairs to create interior archways (see *Hiding Places*, page 60).

• Coffered ceilings in intriguing, waffle-iron patterns can be made with wood strips.

• Arched ceilings can be made of cove planks from a lumber store (see

Below the City, page 22). Barrel vaults can be fabricated from cardboard mailing tubes.

• For an interesting ceiling, use a bubble-surfaced, plastic disposable paint-

Front façade, MANGIA, 1995. Private collection.

HONG KONG / MIAMI, 1994.
19 x 12 x 13 inches. Private
Collection. *This piece was
commissioned to commemorate
the harmonious business relationship between a company's
executives in two cities. The
Chinese gate was built out of a
wind-chime from Chinatown.*

tray liner. The liner can be left as is or
spray-painted any color you choose.

• Skylights can be made by cutting
a section out of the top of a roombox
(see *Jnaneshwar*, page 48). Make a sky-
light window of wood and Plexi, and
build it up out of the box at a slant. Then
add mullions made from thin draftsman's
tape, or very thin wood strips. Use plastic
hemispheres, available in crafts shops, to
make bubble domes.

• If electrifying your scene, consider
installing a ceiling light. If your scene is
not wired, you can make nonworking
lights of buttons and beads, or some

other fixture, like a wagon-wheel cande-
labrum (see *Medieval Hall*, page 90).

• If your scene calls for it, you can
add electrical conduits along the ceiling.
Pipelines can be made from thin metal or
plastic tubing, wood dowels, or flexible
drinking straws. They can be painted or
not, and placed either flush against the
ceiling or slightly below it, wall-to-wall.

• It's easy to make a ceiling fan (see
Miami Beach Bungalow, page 82) out of
wood strips mounted to a golf tee or
short block of wood. Working ceiling
fans are available in dollhouse shops for
electrified rooms.

MEDALLIONS

Medallions are a wonderful way to add design interest to a ceiling. There are several different methods of making medallions. Small wooden plaques can be painted to look like plaster medallions. You can also use wood medallion ornaments, plastic decorative shapes (see *Lost in Time*, below), fancy tin plates or drink coasters, ornate brooches, even doilies treated with glue and fixative. Use a tacky glue to adhere the medallion to the center of the ceiling. A "fresco" painting, chandelier or other lamp can then be added to the center of the medallion. Other sources of medallions are inexpensive plastic plaster molds, available in crafts shops. Alternatively, you can use the molds to make real miniature plaster medallions.

MASTER BEDROOM from THE MINIATURE MANSION, MacKenzie-Childs, 1998. *This series began when Heather MacKenzie-Childs had the idea to dress the windows for Christmas with miniaturized versions of the furnishings in her parents' store. The furniture was reproduced one-quarter the size of the real furniture (salesman's sample size) and came to be displayed as an entire miniature house. In the Master Bedroom, shown here, the ceiling is swathed in gold organza gathered at the center by a medallion, from which a birdcage hangs.*

Detail, LOST IN TIME, 1995. 16 x 14 x 9½ inches. Private collection.

WINDOWS

In *Aloft* (left), I constructed a street scene outside of the box, visible through the windows from the inside. The scene was made out of model-train components and a six-inch replica of the Empire State Building. The Plexi in the window is translucent, to obscure the vista and create an illusion of distance, mystery, and realism. As an alternative, you might attach a scenic photograph behind the pane, as in *North Light* (below), and in the paned door of Tim Prythero's *Kitchen* (right). In *Ann's Calligraphy Studio* (page 28), a second wall at the back of the box provides room for the narrow slice of yard visible through the window. John Mackiewicz

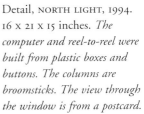

constructed an evocative evening scene out a window in *Room with a View* (page 46).

KITCHEN, Tim Prythero, 1983. 9½ x 12½ x 5 inches. Photo © Gerald Peters. Courtesy O.K. Harris, New York. *This intimate interior, an unusual subject for Prythero, is a rendition of his grand-mother's kitchen.*

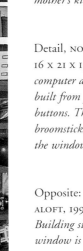

Detail, NORTH LIGHT, 1994. 16 x 21 x 15 inches. *The computer and reel-to-reel were built from plastic boxes and buttons. The columns are broomsticks. The view through the window is from a postcard.*

Opposite:
ALOFT, 1992. *The Empire State Building silhouetted outside the window is a metal souvenir.*

WINDOW STYLES

There's no need to limit yourself to run-of-the-mill rectangular windows. Here are a few ideas for varying your window designs:

• *For diamond-shaped mullions,* see *Vuillard* (page 79); the window was made by painting a plastic soap dish. You might also find plastic baskets with diamond-patterned sides.

• To make a *stained glass window* (right), draw the design on the Plexiglas window with liquid leading, and tint with glass stains (both products are available in arts and crafts stores).

• *Premade sash windows* (working and nonworking) and varieties of bay windows are available from miniatures suppliers. These can be painted, stained, weathered, and decorated. Bay windows allow for window-seats.

• You can make *casements* from the plastic altar-niches found in religious-supplies stores.

STAINED GLASS, 1990. 14 X 23 X 9 inches. *This bedchamber, one of my first dioramas, is built into a bookshelf. The walls are papier-mâché. The steel table was made of notebook rings and masonry nails. The girder on the left was made of tile separators.*

WINDOW TREATMENTS

Following are ideas for creating various window treatments:

• *Curtains:* Run patterned cocktail napkins through a glue-bath (see page 97 for complete instructions).

• *Cafe curtains:* Use shelf edging.

• *Valences:* Use wire-edged ribbon (can also be used for stair carpeting).

• *Paper shades:* Try tack cloth, cross stitch fabric, and mailing tape.

• *Rattan shades:* Try sushi rollers, cocktail coasters, or thin straw matting.

• *Louvered shutters* are available in dollhouse stores. In *Ann's Calligraphy Studio* (page 28), I cut the louvers in half to make short shutters.)

• *Venetian blinds:* Use coffee stirrers.

• *Security gates:* Use fine chicken-wire.

• *Screens:* Use fine mesh (as in a flyswatter). (Arts and crafts stores sell fine-gauge copper and metal "wire mesh." Very fine wire mesh can also can be used for making armatures for anything from tiny sculpture to miniature mountains.)

D O O R S

Doors are powerful elements, the means of entry or escape. Their significance is increased when they imply more than what meets the eye—the existence of rooms beyond.

• For interest, fit a homemade door with a transom.

• Jalousies (see *Miami Beach Bungalow*, below) are easily made by scoring a piece of Plexiglas with a straight-edge and an awl or stylus.

• To make a nonworking door, simply glue a door-frame made from scrap wood to a wall (see *Jnaneshwar's Dream*, page 48). Finish with a knob (a map tack or similar), molding, panels, or other details.

• Consider fitting a door with a gilded arch, an ornamental pediment, or

Detail, MIAMI BEACH BUNGALOW, 1995. 15 x 18 x 29 inches. Private collection.

NEW YORK LAW OFFICE, 1994. 14 x 16 x 13 inches. Private collection. *I applied the name to the door by slipping a typed name, photocopied on clear Mylar, between two layers of textured Plexi.*

MEDIEVAL HALL, 1993. 10 x 45 x 30 inches.

a stone or brick surround. Try making a doorway arch from a fancy plastic party plate: cut the plate into a frame to fit over the door. Spray paint the frame any color and glue it to the wall. Follow the same method to make doorway arches from plastic coffee container lids.

• Make decorative moldings to place around doorways and along walls. Buy a length of woven trim (or braided edging) from a sewing store. Glue it to a strip of wood, and spray evenly with a matte paint. Add thin balsa strips for extra texture.

• Office doors with wavy glass (see *New York Law Office*, above) can be made from textured Plexiglas, available in architectural-model shops. The same kind of door can be fitted with stained or etched glass of your own design. Self-adhesive frosted "privacy screens" for windows can be used to resemble etched glass.

• A heavy, paneled, medieval door (see *Medieval Hall*, left) can be made of scraps of wood. Fittings are dollhouse hardware, clock-hands from a hobby shop, jewelry findings, or shapes cut out of thin metal.

• Miniature doors in different architectural styles are available from dollhouse suppliers. Some possibilities are louver doors, Dutch doors, and French doors. French doors can be single or double, and hung with curtains (see *Uptown Living Room*, page 82).

OFFICE SUPPLIES

• *Pencil jar and pencils:* Paint pencil leads yellow to look like pencils. Put a drop of glue in a "jar" made from a tiny box or bottle top—my favorites are the metal caps of colored pencils, which slip off easily, and the diamond-shaped tops of pencil-lead dispensers.

• *Paperweight:* Stick down a clear plastic "bump" (furniture protector) onto a small colorful designs from a magazine, photo, or postcard. (Another use of these bumpers is for clock-faces—stick one on top of a frontal photo of a clock or watch.)

• *Water cooler:* Make a water cooler from a blue-ink bottle. Leave half a drop of ink to tint the water, and attach it upside down to a plastic box sprayed gray.

• *Waste pail:* The tops of large felt-tip pens make good office waste pails, as do creamer containers.

• *Steel shelving:* From a model train shop, buy a pack of factory windows that come anchored on sprues. Paint the entire kit—windows and sprues—with "chrome" waterbased paint or metallic spray paint. When the paint has dried, snip the sprues from the bottoms of each section of windows. Bend the windows up to a 90° angle, like shelves. Put a dot of glue in the front left and right corner squares of each shelf. Reinforce the shelves with front "legs" made from either chrome-painted ⅛-inch lengths of square brass (available in art and model supply stores), or wood strips, which will fit through the front corners on each side of the shelving unit.

• *Desk pad:* Desk pads of any size can be made by cutting small strips of paper in any color (for example, use pink for phone messages). Fold the strips in half. With a small hand-held stapler, staple the pages together, as close to the top as possible. Flip the first page tightly over the pad and stick it down at the back with double-stick tape.

• *Briefcases and small valises:* Find or cut rectangles of foam rubber (like cosmetic sponges). Cover the foam with book cloth or duct tape. For the handle, pierce the center top with a few unused staples. The cases can be decorated with hardware.

Above:
THE D.A.'S OFFICE, 1991. 10½ x 38½ x 33 inches. *The console is a lacquered chopstick holder. The Venetian blinds were made from a sushi-roller.*

TABLE TABLEAUX

Tables are easy, composed as they are of a top and a base or legs. Ready-made tables can be supported with bases made of candleholders, chess pieces, and napkin rings. You can make the table top from a round or oval lacquer box top, the top or bottom of a square plastic box, or a dollhouse door.

SAMPLE TABLES.
Photo: D. James Dee.

Table legs can be made from wood, plastic, or metal sticks. Shown below are various types of tables made from everyday things:

• *Formica desk and metal filing cabinet:* Instructions are provided below.

• *Formica bedside table and side table:* Plastic boxes and tops

• *Living room lamp-table and low, round coffee tables:* Lacquer box tops

• *Console table:* Scrap wood and gerbil sticks

• *Long coffee table:* Scrap of wood placed upon a base of terra-cotta tile

• *Rustic round table:* A small section of a pine tree trunk

THE LITTLE THINGS

• The *file folders* were cut out of buff card stock. The legal pad is made from a few pages of a small self-adhesive notepad.

• The *pink receipts* are price stickers from a pricing gun. (I begged them from a salesman at the art supplies store.)

• To make the *phone book*, I stood on a ladder and took a picture of the real thing, laid open face down, to get both back and front covers. Once the film was developed, I cut out the cover and inserted yellow self-adhesive notes for pages.

• Cut an inexpensive pocket telephone/address book (available in stationery stores) into miniature

"leather-bound" books. The scale of the vinyl or cardboard is correct, as is the thickness of the pages. The scraps left over can be used to make wallets, desk-blotter corners, belts, handbags, and shoe trim.

• To make a *spiral-bound notebook*, glue the tiny spring found inside a ballpoint pen to the top of a mini self-adhesive notepad.

• Use a black metal paper clamp (binder) from a stationer's to make a *medical bag*. Remove the handles, then cover the clamp with black tape or book cloth. Make satchel handles out of black tape. To finish, cover cardboard triangles with black tape and adhere to each side.

FORMICA DESK

Office furniture can be made in various ways. For *Edward Hopper* (page 71), I made two desks by gluing together scraps of wood. I detailed the desks with bits of molding and trim, then finished with a coat of shellac. The "formica" desk described below is made from plastic paper clip dispensers and a scrap of wood. Follow the same steps to make a "metal" file cabinet.

BASIC TECHNIQUE

1. From the styrene, cut two identical 1¼-inch squares for the file drawers, and two identical ½ x 1¼-inch rectangles for the pencil drawers.

2. Glue the styrene "drawers" onto the front of each box. Glue metal page-markers on the "drawers" for the hardware.

YOU WILL NEED:

Two plastic accessory boxes (such as paper-clip dispensers), approximately 3 inches high by 1½ inches wide
Metal page-markers from stationer's (or similar)
Styrene sheets in white, black, and/or gray
Dollhouse door (without doorframe) or comparable scrap of wood (for desktop)
Miniature-scale half-round molding (optional; for a finished edge)
Scissors
Quick Grab glue

(Staples from a heavy-duty staple-gun can make drawer pulls.)

3. Set the boxes about 2¼ inches apart. Dot the tops with Quick Grab glue, and glue on the wooden desktop. Make sure the desktop is square and even.

Detail, THE KITCHEN FROM THE MINIATURE MANSION, MacKenzie-Childs, 1998. *The base of this fanciful table is handpainted majolica—as is all of the dinnerware—and the tabletop is glass. The pulls on the kitchen drawers complement the fish-back chairs.*

SETTING THE TABLE

Opposite:
Detail, interior counter,
MANGIA, 1995. 25 x 18 x 36
inches. Private collection.
A restaurant on 57th Street.

CLOSE-UP OF A TABLE MADE
OF FOUND OBJECTS. *The cups
are pencil-tops and the plates
are the liners inside soda bottle-
tops.* Photo: D. James Dee.

You'll need food and beverages to make your kitchen and dining room tables inviting. Here are some ideas:

• *Glass of water or milk:* Fill a miniature drinking glass with clear-drying craft glue. It will dry to look like oxygenated tap water, just visible enough to see that the glass is full. If you use white-pigmented craft glue, it will look like milk.

• *Orange juice:* Squeeze a bit of carpenter's wood glue into a miniature glass. The glue dries to the color of orange juice.

• *Candy:* Striped paper clips make old-fashioned stick-candy and candy canes. To make peppermint candy, cut a thin red-and-white striped cocktail straw into thinner sections.

• *Coke can:* With tin-snips or scissors, cut out the two drawings of Coke bottles on aluminum Coca Cola® cans, and the small Coca Cola logos. Follow the border and you'll have the perfect size to roll into a miniature can. Glue the edges together with Quick Grab glue. Cut out a small circle from the same can and use the undecorated side to make a lid.

• *Cookies:* Thin cork from coasters or furniture protectors, cut into disks, make realistic bran cookies. To add "chocolate chips," dot the cookies with a fine, black felt-tip pen.

• *Coconuts:* Cherry pits make plausible coconuts.

• *Hamburgers:* Tiny, rough-textured black rubber dots (available in hardware stores) look just like burgers.

• *Dinner plates:* Use the blue plastic lining in plastic soda bottle caps to make dinner plates.

• *Starched table napkins*: To make napkins, fold wide white tape over upon itself until the right thickness is achieved. Then snip the tape to the desired length. These napkins will glue to a table more easily than cloth will.

• *Drink coasters:* Use small cork dots, available in hardware stores.

• *Salt & pepper dispensers:* Earring posts become salt and pepper shakers. The salt shaker can be turned one way, the pepper shaker the other, to look like a set.

LINENS AND THINGS

A ROOM AT THE INN, 1995. 10 X 12 X 10 inches. Private collection. *I made the gauzy yellow curtains and folded blanket from tack cloth, a product used to remove dust and other debris from painted and varnished surfaces. This sticky fabric has a heavy drape that is well suited to miniatures. The green velvet pillows were adapted from bath sachets.*

The magnificent *Queen Mary's Dolls' House* in Windsor Castle is one of the most famous miniatures in the world. It was designed by Sir Edwin Lutyens, the architect of the city of New Delhi. Everything in it works—the rifles can be loaded, the pipes smoked, the lift operated, and the water actually runs. Nevertheless, despite all of its realism, a tablecloth sticks out unnaturally because it isn't heavy enough to hang properly. In a written study, Clifford Musgrave addresses the difficulty of working with textiles in miniature: "Materials behave in a different way when used on a small scale. Fabrics. . .although made of the finest and most delicate materials, seem to be unusually stiff. . . ."

Observe the heft and drape of any fabrics you plan to render in small scale. For example, pillows should flop heavily, not swell like balloons. Sometimes very thin cotton works, as in the bedclothes in *The Steamship* (page 59), but beware of linens that billow out like hoop skirts. For curtains, towels, blankets, and sheets, I often run paper towels and napkins run through a glue-bath (opposite, below).

TO MAKE A GLUE BATH

Combine equal parts white craft glue and water in a shallow baking pan; mix to the consistency of cream. Trim the paper towel or napkin to size. Hold the napkin by one end and carefully drag it through the glue-bath until saturated. Allow the excess glue mixture to drip off into the pan. Gently position the napkin in place, then manipulate into gathers or folds, as desired.

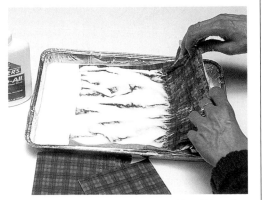

Photo: D James Dee.

LOFT INTERIOR, 1992. 16 x 21 x 15 inches. *The blue afghan tossed over the arm of the sofa was taken from a worn-out flannel pillowcase that had been washed to just the right drape.*

A RATHER MESSY BED

To make the bedclothes in the sample project, I used paper napkins run through a glue-bath (page 97). In addition to paper napkins, women's lingerie often works for bedclothes, particularly pure silk. When using patterned fabrics, consider using the reverse side: as scale diminishes, so does color. Even with a small-enough pattern, colors that are too bright will detract from the realism.

YOU WILL NEED:

One 3½ x 5½-inch cellulose sponge (or similar object, like a blackboard eraser)

1 piece balsa or other soft wood, same size as sponge, about ½-inch thick

4 pushpins

Printed paper napkins

Tea bags or silicone packing inserts (for pillows)

White craft glue

2 shallow, disposable aluminum baking pans, or similar

Jigsaw, coping or razor saw, or X-Acto knife (to cut wood)

Sample of a "messy bed."
Photo: D. James Dee.

BASIC TECHNIQUE

1. With scissors, trim the top edges of the sponge to soften the angles, so that the "linen" will realistically cover the "mattress."

2. Glue the bottom of the sponge to the wood scrap.

3. Fix pushpins into the bottom corners of the wood to make the legs of the bed.

4. Stand the bed in one of the shallow pans. In the other pan, make a glue-bath by combining equal parts white craft glue and water. Stir the mixture to the consistency of cream.

5. Decide on a napkin to use for the bottom sheet. Lay the dry napkin over the bed, and trim the excess. (I prefer the sheet to line up with the headboard of the bed, but reach the floor on both sides and at the foot.)

6. Carefully drag the napkin through the glue-bath. Hold the saturated napkin over the pan to allow the excess glue to drip off. Transfer the napkin to the bed. As you place it down, the napkin will automatically form wrinkles in perfect scale. Gently manipulate and sculpt the napkin to create a draping or bunching effect, as desired. But, be careful—wet napkins tear easily.

7. If desired, repeat the procedure to make a top sheet and blanket. As you place the bedclothes on the bed, stagger the layers so that each is visible. If desired, fold a blanket (while still damp) at the foot of the bed.

8. There are various ways to make pillows. You can cover a damp teabag with a napkin that's been through a glue bath, or you can simply spray-paint a teabag. Desiccant packing-inserts are good for making boudoir-pillows. If you sew a pillow, use very thin cloth, and fill it with sand rather than with cotton: pillows are heavy, and should look so. The impression from a very small spoon will give a pillow the indentation of a head.

TRY THIS

Make small picture frames from watchband buckles. If a very tiny frame is needed, cut out a rectangle from a plastic basket and paint it gold or silver. Glue a tiny photograph (from a snapshot or a magazine ad) to the back of the frame. Make a picture "stand" out of cardboard for use on a table, mantel, or piano.

THE LITTLE THINGS

• The *tall cabinet* is a wooden toothbrush-box. The nightstand is a Christmas-tree ornament, and the small photo frame is a picture hook. I used Indian bindis to make the jewelry.

• The *wallpaper* is made from giftwrap; the carpet is a fabric sample. The throw rug is a tobacco-company souvenir found at a flea market.

• The bed's *headboard* is made from a decorative wood appliqué; the footboard is made from carpenter's molding. You can also use thin picture-frame molding or brass findings, drawer pulls, and hinges.

• The *framed painting* is a color photocopy of a self-portrait. You could also cut out a detail from a family or vacation snapshot, or a postcard print of a painting by a favorite artist, to personalize a setting.

• The *miniature afghan* is made by peeling mini terracotta bricks from their mesh backing, then coloring the mesh with felt-tip pens. If you place a piece of paper beneath the mesh as you color, some interesting graphic designs, like florets in repeat-patterns, will appear. This paper can be used as miniature gift-wrap or wallpaper.

CLOTHING

One of the pleasures of this art form is morphing banal objects into utterly different things. Here are a few tips on how to "fake" clothing:

• *Ski caps:* Snip off the fingertips of wool gloves, turn up the brim.

• *Scarf:* Can be made from an "amigo band" (a handwoven friendship bracelet).

• *Hangers:* Shape vinyl-coated paper clips with a needle-nose pliers.

• *Shoes:* An eyeglass repair kit comes with two nose-pads, useful for making shoe soles. Add cloth to the toe to make scuffs, or to the toe and heel to make espadrilles. Use a thread thong to make sandals. Another approach is to notch either side of the "sole" with a needle. Thread the needle with embroidery floss and draw it through the sticky side of the pad, toward the front. Hook the floss

into the notches-one side at a time, over the back, then up through the other notch-it will look like a toe thong. To hide the threads on the bottom, stack the sole on a second sticky-backed nose-pad.

• *Clothes in stacks:* Cut and fold thin cotton socks and T-shirts to make stacks of sweaters, blankets, towels, etc. for closet shelves. You can use baby terrycloth washcloths for towels. Keep in mind that worn fabric has better drape, hue, and weight

for miniature scale. Front and back sides of some fabrics offer variety of weaves that can add textural interest. Rolling-pin sheathes have a tiny-scale weave, ideal for miniatures. Glue stacks of folded cloth with tacky glue.

• *Hats:* Cut out a circle of nylon strapping for the hat brim and glue on a small half-round or other shape (such as half a plastic ball, or the bottom of a disposable plastic creamer). A bit of embroidery floss will make a hatband. A feather can be found from a goose-feather pillow, or clip a piece of feather from a feather duster.

Above:
TELEVISION STUDIO: WARDROBE DEPARTMENT, 1991. 32 X 34 X 14 inches. *One view of a 360-degree diorama inspired by the television series* Beauty and the Beast.

IN THE BATH

Found objects can also be used to accessorize a mini bathroom.

• Make a *tub mat* by cutting a small piece from a rubber, jar-opening "lid twist."

• Plastic bags, especially the translucent recycling trash bags, make good *shower curtains.*

• To make a *straw hamper,* glue a dark shade of nylon strapping around a dental floss container or other small box. Cut a lid from cardboard, hinge it with a simple fold, and glue it on. Emphasize the "weave" by lightly spraying the strap with white paint. To make the "straw" look more rigid, spray with fixative or clear varnish.

• Katharine Forsyth grimed up her miniature bathroom (below) by spattering diluted waterbased paint onto the fixtures. For a bathtub ring, the tub was filled with diluted black paint and allowed to sit overnight. The ring remained after the paint was poured out. The faucets were painted black and wiped repeatedly until the desired effect was reached.

BATHROOM, Katharine Forsyth, 1999. 10¾ x 9 x 9 inches. *This diorama was built into a commercial corner-box, with a curving, flexible Plexi front. The container can be used horizontally or vertically, and is a nice change from the typical rectangular roombox.*

PRACTICE ROOMS

Here are two simple how-to projects, made with common materials, that are intended to help get your feet wet and your hands full of paint and glue. As informal exercises in creativity, they're meant to introduce the improvisational uses of simple tools and materials, and experiments with abstraction, design, color, composition, and scale. You can treat these projects like recipes and modify them to taste. Once the principles become familiar, the themes can be endlessly varied.

A VALENTINE COTTAGE

This four-room cottage-in-the-round can be a table centerpiece or mobile. The Valentine-theme rooms (bedroom, dining room, den, garden parlor) were made with inexpensive, everyday materials. Once you've gathered the materials, it will take only a couple of hours to complete the house.

Two views of the VALENTINE COTTAGE. 2001.

YOU WILL NEED:

One 12-inch-square piece of foam core
Two 9 x 12-inch pieces of foam core
X-Acto knife and #11 blades
Scissors
Self-adhesive notepad
Steel T-square ruler
Waterbase hobby paints in various colors
Hobby paintbrushes
Approximately ½-inch-wide edging tape
    (cloth book-tape or white art tape) to
    trim the outer edges of the walls
Thematic details (in this case, hearts from
    charms, beads, stickers, confetti, jewelry)
White craft glue (Elmer's or Tacky) and
    Quick Grab
Thin wood stripping, half rounds (beading),
    quarter rounds, and chair-rail molding
    (optional)
Small cosmetic mirror(s)
Felt scraps or textile swatches for rugs
Origami paper (patterned)
Tiny plastic or cardboard boxes
Valentine cards to cut up for wall-art
Paper doilies and fancy napkins

BASIC TECHNIQUE

Work on all four rooms at once, in stages: paint all of the floors at the same time, then proceed to wallpapering the walls, etc.

I. On the 12-inch-square piece of foam core (the base), draw a line down the center and a line across to make four equal 6-inch-square floors (see *Fig. 1*). Identify each square: "den," "bedroom," "dining room," "garden parlor"; attach a self-adhesive note to the underside of each floor as a readable tag.

2. Paint the four floors as you like— all the same color, diagonal floors in contrasting colors and patterns, etc. You could also cover each floor with patterned paper or sheets of styrene tile.

3. Draw a line down the middle of the 9 x 12-inch piece of foam core, on both the front and back. This will determine the boundary of each wall.

4. Cut the other 9 x 12-inch piece of foam core in half to make two 6 x 9-inch pieces for the remaining two walls (see *Fig. 2*).

5. On the uncut 9 x 12-inch piece of foam core, mark and then excise two doorways, each about 1½ inches wide by 4 inches high (see *Fig. 3*). The waste pieces can be used for the doors, which are attached later. If desired, paint the doors, or apply door-moldings, which can be made of wood or cardboard strips or simply drawn on.

6. When the floors have dried, set the walls up but do not glue them in place.

DETAILS

You can paper walls and other surfaces with interesting giftwrap or handmade, textured papers. Spray-mount the paper to the surface, or use wallpaper glue. Smooth the paper in place to avoid ripples and air pockets. See pages 76–79 for other decorating ideas.

Fig. 1.

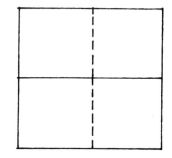

Fig. 2.

Fig. 3.

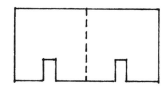

Fig. 4.

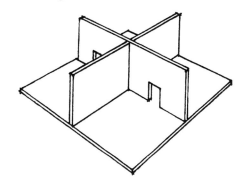

Label each adjacent wall of each room with a self-adhesive note: "bedroom," "den," "garden parlor," "dining room." (This is so you can disassemble the walls and lay them flat to work on.)

7. Paint or cover the walls with Origami or other paper for all four rooms. (*Note:* The straightest edges should be glued together for the best fit; the less perfect edges should be on the outside. You can use trim—balsa strips, tape, etc.—to hide imperfections.) To paper and/or paint the walls, lay the two halves of a room together, flat on a table. Decorate each pair of walls one room at a time, so that, when set up at right angles, the wall decorations are aligned.

8. When all of the walls are decorated, glue the 9 x 12-inch piece of foam core perpendicularly to the floor with Quick Grab or Tacky Bond. Glue on the two 6 x 9-inch perpendicular walls (see *Fig. 4*). Hold the walls in place until the glue sets.

9. If desired, glue on the two doors. Consider leaving them partially open to give a peek into the next room. Doorknobs can be made of map tacks, beads, earring-posts, and the like.

10. Trim the outer edges of the walls and floor with tape, wrapping the edges to hide unevenness and the foam core layers.

11. Furnish the rooms with handmade furniture, fireplace, shelves, table, benches. Add details, such as framed pictures, books, food, table settings, mirrors, etc. (see "The Little Things," below).

12. If you wish for this piece to hang as a mobile, attach a hook and wire or string to the top. Finish the bottom of the base with Origami or other paper.

TRY THIS

Make a floppy, wrinkled bed pillow from a used teabag. While the teabag is damp, spray-paint it any color. Bolsters can be made from the fingers of leather gloves. If the glove is lined, no stuffing will be required.

THE LITTLE THINGS

For the Bedroom: In this sample, the bed is a small box. The rug is plastic strapping from a lawn chair. If desired, you can make a rustic rug from a bootlace or a length of thick yarn by winding it in a snug circle or oval and gluing it to paper. The shelves here are craft sticks. The bulletin board is a piece of flat cork. You could make a lamp from a small lamp finial, and a shade from a toothpaste tube top or a plastic creamer top.

For the Den: Make a fireplace from a small rectangular box or tiny picture frame. Paint a piece of wadded tape with fluorescent paint for a fire. The wainscoting is a piece of brown corrugated paper. (Fine-scale corrugated paper comes in light-bulb packaging.) The sofa is the bottom of a paper box, cut in half. The candlesticks are wood screws.

For the Dining Room: Make a dining table from a box top, jar lid, or from coffee-stirrers glued together. The base can be a spool, short dowel, plastic box, domino, or a few dice. The benches are craft sticks supported by gameboard tiles. The valentine candy is made from red and pink beads; you could also cut up a red plastic straw or coffee stirrer. The valentine cake is a sugar cake-decoration from a bakery supplies store.

For the Garden Room: The planting table is a small square box top. The cartons are wood blocks covered with packing tape. The bag of potting soil is actually coffee grounds in cellophane. The pot is a thimble, and the tool bucket is the top of a lipstick container. The slippers are eyeglass nose-pads. The spade is from a plastic drink stirrer.

A FIREPLACE ROOM

I made the demonstration fireplace (opposite) in a 9 x 11 x 5 inch produce box. The framed picture on the mantel is a photo of my newborn nephew Joe. A box like this would make an original new-baby gift!

BASIC TECHNIQUE

To Make a Fireplace

1. With a jigsaw, saw off one of the two long sides of the frame, so that you're left with a three-sided upside down U-shape.

2. Mount the fireplace on the backing, making sure that both tops are square and level.

3. To hide unevenness, cover the bottom of the fireplace legs with wood painted stone or slate.

4. Glue the mantel and the mirror to the backboard.

Opposite:
SAMPLE FIREPLACE.
Photo: D. James Dee.

Below:
Detail, FLORINE STETTHEIMER,
THE BALLROOM, 1996.
12 x 18½ x 8 inches (entire structure). *I made this mantel from a scrap of wood and a mitered piece of a fancy picture frame. I added a wooden base and a wooden back painted black. The decorations on the surround are metal ornaments from a scrap-metal store.*

YOU WILL NEED:

Produce or other similar-sized box
Picture frame, approximately 3 x 5 inches, with the glass and back removed
Piece of wood or thick foam core, approximately 6 x 1 inches (for the mantel)
Scrap molding in assorted patterns (from a dollhouse store)
A purse-size cosmetic mirror (or triangular mirrors from a crafts store)
Scrap wood backboard, approximately 5 x 8 inches, painted to look like slate
Fluorescent acrylic paints in orange, red, yellow, and blue
Jigsaw
Quick Grab glue
Disposable plastic plate or sheet of Plexiglass
Plastic knife
Single-edge razor or glass scraper
Scissors
Twigs, gravel, or small stones

To Make a Fire

1. Onto a disposable plastic plate or sheet of glass or Plexi, squeeze out fluorescent acrylics: orange, red, yellow, and blue. Brush them thickly on the glass with a plastic knife, as if mixing colors for a painting. Let the colors dry.

2. With a single-edge razor or glass scraper, remove the wad of dried acrylic paint, which will be rubbery enough to allow for shaping with a scissors. Add additional touches of color, if desired.

3. Glue the "fire" inside the fireplace on twigs or miniature "coals." (To make "burning" coals: Lightly spray black aquarium gravel or small black and gray pebbles with fluorescent orange paint.)

THE LITTLE THINGS

- The *candles* are painted nails.
- The *kindling box* is an incense holder.
- The *floor mat* is a sample from a book of industrial fabrics.
- The *wallpaper* is wrapping paper.
- The *gold box* on the mantel is a locket.
- The *silver dollhouse* is a tea-infuser (available in a housewares store).
- The *geode* is a real geode, from a gemstone store.

- The *little red house* is from a Monopoly® game.
- The *folk-art doll* (a handmade pin) and the Mexican crèche are both from museum shops.
- The *music stand* is an antique razor.
- The *pictures* to the left of the doll and the music stand are magnets.
- The two *bookcases* on the right are Christmas-tree ornaments.
- The *brass vase* is a bullet cartridge!

EXTERIORS

Simulate the many known exterior textures, or improvise your own creative façades. Use an extra tacky glue or a strong glue like Quick Grab to adhere the surface treatments.

• Make roofs of tin, copper, or other sheet metal. Apply a collage of tree bark to a roof.

• Make your own shingles or roof tiles by cutting them out of balsa strips or coarse sandpaper. Spanish tiles can be made from drinking straws cut length-

DAISY QUEEN, Tim Prythero, 1991. 17 x 36 x 20 inches. Photo © Gerald Peters. Courtesy O.K. Harris Works of Art, New York. *At first glance, one is struck by the elegant symmetry and sculptural shape of the building. On closer inspection, the distressed, weathered façade reveals a deeper level of narrative content.*

Exterior, SARASTRO'S EGYPTIAN ROOM (TEMPLE OF DENDUR) from THE MAGIC FLUTE series, 1997–99. 20 x 18 x 18 inches. *The Masonite edifice was built by a woodworker from specs I supplied.*

wise. False fingernails will work too. Consider tiling a roof with small seashells, available in crafts stores.

• Apply split logs (made from small branches) to the exterior of a log cabin. Create a "Tudor" look with beams. Make clapboard siding out of balsa wood strips.

• One way to make corrugated metal siding is simply to spray corrugated cardboard with aluminum paint. Another way is to use heavy metal foil scribed with a stylus and straight edge, or with a comb.

• Make "stucco" walls with plaster or spackling compound. Apply pebbles to spackling compound for stone walls.

• Weather painted exterior walls by rubbing stains or thinned paints lightly over the façade.

• There are different ways to make a brick façade. You can buy styrene sheets of brick, as I did on *Balcony, Uptown Living Room* (below). This was an early diorama and I didn't realize that I could have made the bricks look more realistic (and more interesting) by varying their colors with paint. There are also specialty papers available that are printed and embossed with brick patterns. For even greater realism, there are miniature bricks that come on a mesh backing that you can grout with spackling compound.

Balcony, UPTOWN LIVING ROOM, 1991. 12 x 36 x 36 inches. *The wall paintings are segments of an Impressionist painting postcard. The art on the bedroom wall was taken from the soft-focus background of a magazine fashion shot. The glass étagères are made of Plexi, and the African sculpture assembled from a cigar stem and bamboo cocktail fork.*

DISTRESSING NEWS

KIT BASHING, WEATHERING, AND AGING

Bashing and distressing are destructive-sounding terms for the magical techniques of altering, rebuilding, or texturing components. Distressing is the process of artificially deteriorating the appearance of something new to make it look old, weathered, worn out, well-used, or abused. Kit-bashing refers to the modification of kits or mass-produced dollhouse furniture. With kit-bashing, artists can transform a commercial object into a one-of-a-kind piece, or use readymade components to create an object otherwise difficult to fabricate. In *Bus Station* (below), John Mackiewicz "cannibalized" plastic bathtub kits and refashioned them into waiting-room chairs. Another example is when he glues or laminates layers upon layers of components to fabricate luncheonette-style coffee urns out of model car parts.

Why would anyone wish to turn a shiny, new one-inch-scale table into the semblance of a shabby ruin? Answer: To carry off the illusion of realism, fabricate deception, fantasize the factual, and imprint an uninspiring object with verve. A generic dollhouse table looks like a standard, new, nondescript toy, but you can make that table bear the fascinating evidence of hard use and the passage of time with chipped paint, age-stains, gouges, and other hints of use and abuse. Every artist has his own methods. Tim Prythero says that weathering and aging effects should be built up in layers. His *14th*

Opposite:
FOUND OBJECTS, 1996.
22 x 13 x 10 inches. *An artist's studio, made out of found objects, about making art out of found objects.*

BUS STATION, John Mackiewicz, 1991. 12 x 18 x 14 inches. Courtesy O.K. Harris Works of Art, New York. *Beyond the grimy glass doors is a large bus. This piece began with the construction of three-quarters of a one-inch-scale bus. The pay phone is scratch-built from odds and ends. The lettering for CAFETERIA is from a stencil set, the letters cut out individually and glued to a piece of neon-red Plexi that's back-lit. There are two six-inch fluorescent fixtures in the ceiling; the one with a blue filter illuminates the bus outside the terminal and indicates night. The interior fluorescent was left untreated by gels, to give a stark, institutional look.*

Detail, THE STEAMSHIP, 1996.
10 x 13 x 9 inches (entire
structure).

Detail, HIDING PLACES.

and Union (page 42) is not only time-ravaged, but savaged by the wrecking-ball.

John Mackiewicz also ages objects by layering; he applies acrylic paints over spray paint, then rubs on additional layers of paint and stain. Viewers are riveted by the detailed realism of years of grease encrusted on a jerry-rigged luncheonette grill, or the pies that have been malingering in their dingy cooler, and the floorboards and chipped wall tile that look half a century old. In a Mackiewicz, you can sense the place moldering, sinking into itself. You begin to surmise what sort of character might have been sitting at that counter, with its dubious still-life of tepid coffee and stale pie: likely someone lamenting a misspent life. All these subjective intimations, associations, impressions, and tales come from the effects imparted by a ravaged milieu.

I think there's something very satisfying about "ruining" new furniture. The bureau in *The Steamship* (above), and the table in *Hiding Places* (above, left) were once pristine; what fun to rid the furniture of polish through a battery of antiquing techniques. Tim Prythero begins his structures from "a point of newness" and imposes the aging process. "From the effects of weather and time," he says, "the accumulation of clutter and the details left by everyday living, the inanimate object begins to take on a life of its own."

Aside from the antics of distressing and weathering, there's a certain aesthetic beauty that comes from age, such as paint worn down to the wood grain, or rust collecting on metal. The Japanese have a word to describe the surprising, unpredictable beauty of the colors that emerge when glazed ceramics are fired. This not easily translatable word is *shibui*. I like to think of weathering and aging miniature objects as exercises in *shibui*.

Here are some easy methods for getting objects to look worn and contribute rich textures to a miniature scene. You might want to explore home-decorating and paint stores for the many products available for crackling, lime washing, color washing, stippling, and creating patina and verdigris effects.

• A crackle medium works with water-based paints and is easy to use. Simply paint an object with a base color and let it dry. This color will show through the intricate cracks formed after applying crackle and another contrasting color. The furniture will seem to have had many coats of paint applied over the years.

• Alter the appearance of new furniture with fleck paint and patina solutions. Use patina solutions to antique and oxidize bright brass. (See the brass garden ornaments in *Pamina and Monostatus*, page 116.)

- To weather terra-cotta: lightly spray a flowerpot with green spray paint (mold) and/or white spray paint (lime).

- Unevenly sand painted furniture with an emery board or fine sandpaper. Concentrate on the edges, which are particularly vulnerable to wear. You can also burnish polished or painted wood with steel wool.

- In *Times Square Hotel Room* (page 54), Alan Wolfson used modeling paste to stucco the walls. Top an undercoat of dried wall paint with a layer of modeling paste. When the paste dries, burnish with a scouring brush for a scratched look.

- John Mackiewicz uses a diluted ink wash to accentuate shadows in crevices. Fixtures appear to have been there "forever," as if they've sunk a bit into the floor. To get this effect, apply diluted ink shadows where the object contacts the floor.

- There are solutions available in craft and home-decorating stores that will produce verdigris effects. Simulate rust by painting a base coat of waterbased metallic pigment (copper, bronze, etc.), then dabbing the paint dry with an oxidizing color of green or blue-green. To weather further, lightly sponge on dark gray paint.

- One of Mackiewicz's aging tricks is dry-brushing, using a lighter shade of a certain color, or a light earth tone. He dips a brush in paint, then removes most of the paint with a rag until the brush is almost dry. Then he scrubs the brush lightly over the surface to highlight textures and details.

HEARTBREAK HOTEL, John Mackiewicz, 1990. 8 x 10 x 8 inches. Private collection. Courtesy O.K. Harris Works of Art, New York. *Mackiewicz's first piece. A room in which many activities apparently are going on at once "all by implication." The fixtures are a Chrysnbon bathroom kit, distressed.*

LANDSCAPING

Whether your miniature includes a sprout in a sidewalk crack, a formal French garden, or a recreation of Sherwood Forest or Birnam Wood, references to nature embellish a scene with color, texture, and "life." Landscape materials for trees, shrubs, grass, and flowers are available in dollhouse, railroad- and architectural-model shops, but they are often expensive. Over the years I've figured out how to make seasonal foliage using inexpensive everyday materials, as well as borrowing from nature itself.

Tiny hemlock cones translate down into one-inch-scale pinecones. You can dry flowers to crumble for ground cover and leaves; and collect twigs, branches, and tree roots for trees (see *Central Park, Winter*, opposite). Tree armatures can be purchased or made of wire, but I prefer to use branches and twigs. Bushes and foliage can be made from sea sponges, or synthetic sponges cut to shape and painted. Florist's foam, cut to shape, is great for making hedges and bushes, as are loofahs, pieces of foam rubber, steel wool, and scouring pads. Flowers can be made out of polymer clay, or stamped out of paper with a flower-shaped punch. Tiny seashells, pebbles, chipped rocks, gemstones, and even dried beans and seeds can all be successfully incorporated in a landscape.

It's a good idea to have a supply of spongy foam foliage on hand. Foam foliage is available in many colors in crafts and railroad-model stores—keep an assortment of shades to mix together.

I also buy loose "grass" in packets, as well as rolls of readymade lawns. Crafts stores carry a material called "flock" or "flocking," which is useful for creating fine-scale foliage. Common dried herbs can be used for ground cover and topiaries. Landscaping accessories can be easily made: picket or twig fences, garden statuary, lily ponds, stone walls, grottos (papier-mâché studded with bits of rock, shell, and glass), gazebos, trellises, and benches.

Here are ideas for composing the four seasons.

SPRING

Among the principal characters of Mozart's opera, *The Magic Flute*, are Pamina, the princess, who is in love with Tamino, the prince. *Pamina and*

CATHERINE'S BALCONY, 1990. 10½ x 23 x 9½ inches. *This diorama, which was built into a black-painted bookshelf, is an earlier version of the balcony scene pictured on page 109, having the view looking into the apartment. This diorama looks out on the Manhattan skyline, a backdrop painted with acrylics on paper.*

Opposite:
Detail, CENTRAL PARK, WINTER, 1993. 28 x 17 x 10 inches. Private collection. *The trees at the left are roots from a thirty-year-old oak tree felled by a Florida hurricane. The complex root system more effectively simulates tree branches than the twigs on the right do.*

TOPIARY TIPS

Topiaries enliven a landscape with sculptural detail. Follow these basic steps to make topiaries in various shapes and forms.

1. Dab the end of the toothpick or dowel in white glue and insert it into a wooden bead or Styrofoam ball. Snip off any protrusion from the top of the bead. If you plan on using more than one bead, push the first bead a little way down on the dowel.

2. Holding the dry end of the dowel, twirl the bead in a small dish of white glue, then dredge it in model railroad grass, dried herbs, or green foam foliage (also a model railroad item). For thin patches, dab on more white glue or spray mount, and sprinkle on additional grass and/or herbs. Repeat steps to add more beads to the dowel.

3. Fill the flowerpot with clay, florist foam, or papier-mâché, and top with brown paint or a layer of coffee grounds for soil.

4. Snip the dowel stem to the desired length, and glue it into the pot.

Below:
PAMINA AND MONOSTATUS IN THE ROSE BOWER (CONSERVATORY GARDEN, CENTRAL PARK). 23 x 27 x 18 inches. *The 18th-century-style garden ornaments are made of cake baking supplies, place-card holders, and hardware findings. On the Egyptian obelisk, a replica of the real one in Central Park, I scribed hieroglyphs for the words "magic," "flute," and "singing men and women."*

Monostatus (opposite) is set in spring to symbolize Pamina's youth. The garden statuary is made of cake ornaments, sometimes painted gray to resemble stone. The groundcover is medium-green spongy grass sprinkled with light green to suggest new growth. *The Temple of Wisdom / Reason / Nature* (right) is set in spring to indicate Tamino's budding wisdom upon encountering the high priest Sarastro. Again, twigs are foliated with light green strawflowers and plastic leaves interspersed with pink and white buds.

SUMMER

The *Sound of the Magic Flute* (below) takes place in Ft. Tryon Park in upper Manhattan, near the Cloisters. The trees are branches and twigs, with foliage of green-dyed strawflowers and plastic deco-

rative foliage from florists' shops, dime stores, and pet stores. Some of the shrubs

TEMPLE OF WISDOM / REASON / NATURE (NEW YORK PUBLIC LIBRARY). 26 X 27 X 18 inches. *The New York Public Library on 42nd Street and Fifth Avenue has the same colonnade and triple doors that the libretto calls for. I substituted Egyptian for Roman statues on the parapet. After this piece was photographed, I found miniature sphinxes (rubber pencil erasers) to place next to the Library Lions.*

THE SOUND OF THE MAGIC FLUTE (FT. TRYON PARK). 20 X 27 X 12 inches. *The animals are toys, jewelry, tree ornaments, and bibelots.*

All works on these two pages are from THE MAGIC FLUTE series, 1997–99.

1994. 12 x 36 x 24 inches.
*This tableau was set up on a
big table and disassembled
after being photographed. The
carousel was built from a carv-
ing board, two tambourines,
pencils, and a tin pagoda. The
"concrete" wall at the rear is
wine-crate packing. The fence
in the foreground is a chain of
carpenter's nails. The fancy
grillwork under the stone arch
is a tin napkin-holder.*

in *Central Park Carousel* (above) are also
plastic. There are many ways to make a
grassy lawn. For this scene, I first painted
the wood base a neutral, earthy color, then
sprayed with adhesive spray onto which
I sprinkled loose grass, crumbled leaves,
and grass foam in light and medium shades
of green. *Papageno's Nest* (page 20) is set
in full summer to represent the bird-
catcher's full-bodied *joie de vivre* and simple
hedonistic connection with nature. The
birdcages are decorations, charms, toys,
and jewelry. The trees in *Drainage Culvert*
(page 122) were made of twigs and lichen,
and the gravel of sand and cat litter.

FALL

Gramercy Park (page 72) is set in mid-
autumn. For the largest tree, I chose a

branch with true-to-scale knotholes and
limbs. The leaves are strawflowers, available in many colors in florists' shops. The
ground is covered with small stones made
from cat litter and aquarium gravel,
lichen, railroad grass, herbs, and crumbled leaves taken from dried flower stems.
To add a layer of rich color, sprinkle hot
chili flakes over the ground.

I'd place *Death Speaks: The Graveyard
Scene* (opposite, top) in late November.
This was one occasion where I didn't have
to vivify dried foliage—the deader the
better. The tangled knobs of dried grape
stems worked well here. To make the
fallen leaves, I painted a piece of typing
paper (or thin brown Kraft paper) front
and back with watercolors. When completely dry, I punched out the leaf shapes
with a specialty punch, available in stationery and crafts stores. For authenticity,

curl, fold and crumple the paper leaves before scattering them on the ground. Alternatively, you can crumble dried leaves from cut flowers and scatter them on a coat of spray adhesive.

WINTER

Without much foliage, winter is the easiest season to create. In *Frozen Pond* (right), the ice is a piece of transparent, smoky Plexiglas over brown Kraft paper. Snow was built up around it using papier-mâché that was then painted white and sprinkled with baking powder. For a sunny scene, use white glitter to make the snow sparkle. Duco cement will make

DEATH SPEAKS: THE GRAVEYARD SCENE, 2000. 18½ x 25½ x 18 inches. *The statue of the Commandatore is an antique pewter equestrian whose masked and cloaked appearance reflects wrongful death.*

FROZEN POND, 1992. *The park bench was made from wooden coffee stirrers.*

UNDER THE EL, John
Mackiewicz, 1993. 12 x 18 x
14 inches. Courtesy O.K.
Harris Works of Art, New
York. *Mackiewicz used tiny
half-round plastic dolls' eyes
to make the seventy-two rivets
for the El.*

bare branches look ice-covered. The snow
in John Mackiewicz's *Under the El*
(above) was made similarly, with the
addition of a touch of blue acrylic, gloss
medium, and mica particles. The icicles
are silicone caulking detailed with white
paint and gloss medium.

To contribute to the look of coldness
in *The Queen of the Night* (opposite,
below), reflecting the Queen's icy hauteur,
I chose a color scheme of white, black,
blue, and silver. At the foot of the castle
is a ring of plastic iridescent snowflakes
(Christmas decorations). Brambles painted
silver are interspersed with sparkly silver
strawflowers. The backdrop is a sheet of
spangled plastic-coated paper from a
plastics store. Around the scene are scat-
tered blue plastic "rocks" that resemble ice
cubes. To ornament the tower's exterior
and interior, I used buttons and findings

with crescent moons and stars. The silver
arrows (cocktail picks) that felled the
dragon in the opening scene lie on the ice.

SEASONAL
AMBIGUITY

As much as I love the city, I have to
admit that sometimes it's hard to tell what
season it happens to be, unless there's a
nearby tree to examine for clues. Even so,
urban trees aren't always reliable season-
indicators. In a waggish mood, I might
have subtitled *Night Prowl* (page 124)
"Anonymous Lot in an Indeterminate
Season." It could be spring or summer,
with a moribund tree or two. On the
other hand, it could be a snowless winter.
If I wanted to gloss it up as if it had just

rained, I could have sprayed it heavily with a clear varnish. *The Palm Court* (right) is a supernatural scene with trees of silver and gold. This is a miniature of the Wintergarden that once stood at the World Financial Center in lower Manhattan, an enormous glass-walled arboretum sheltering sixteen-foot-tall palm trees. In the miniature, the trunks of the palms were made by winding textured paper resembling bark around wooden dowels. The fringed fronds were cut from thin sheets of tin and heavy-duty aluminum foil.

THE PALM COURT from THE MAGIC FLUTE series, 1997–99. 15 x 15 x 10 inches. Private collection. *I added black-and-white tiles, a Masonic motif, to the rose and gray marble floor of the Wintergarden. The benches, which look like those in the Wintergarden, conform to the specs in the libretto, as do the silver and gold palms. The exposed structure of the arboretum is made from plastic basket grids and metal griddle baskets used in frying.*

GARDEN ORNAMENTS

Consider including ornamental details in your miniature garden. Any of these can be made of found objects.

• Turn a florist's frog upside down to make a *garden table.*

• *Rustic furniture and garden benches* can be constructed of wooden sticks, twigs, smooth stones, or formed of wire.

• Metal finials and other hardware findings can be transformed into mini *stone and iron ornaments and pedestals.*

• *Sundials* can be made out of chess pieces.

• Aquarium gravel, cat litter, pebbles, and dried beans can be used as *paving stones* in tile or gravel paths.

• Construct *arbors* and *trellises* from plastic or wire baskets, balsa wood strips, and twigs.

• Top a wedding cake pedestal with a small, shallow dish to make a *bird bath.* Coil rope to make a small beehive.

• Attach wheels to a plastic scoop to make a *wheelbarrow.*

• *Scarecrows* are easy to shape from straw or raffia.

• Spray a toy figurine with gray primer to make *stone lions* or other animals.

THE QUEEN OF THE NIGHT from THE MAGIC FLUTE series, 1997-99.

GRASS ROOTS LANDSCAPING TIPS

• There's much a miniaturist can do with *floral supplies.* The soft, moldable, porous foam used to anchor plants can be sculpted into shrubs, bushes, and hedges, or used as groundcover or tracts of hilly land. Florist spikes make good picket fences. Glue them flush together or separated by horizontal wood strips. Covered florist wire makes leaves and stems. For green leaves, sandwich florist wire between two layers of adhesive material, such as green duct tape, library tape, or green-painted labels. Cut out the leaf shape, leaving enough wire to twine around a stem.

• Among the many varieties of *dried foliage* that are perfect for miniature scenes are reindeer moss, rice flowers, lace or pepper grass, caspia or mystic, mini asparagus (not to be confused with the vegetable), thatch reed (for miniature bamboo), star flowers, kol kol, miniature *Gypsophila*

(baby's breath), bloom broom, and agrotis (like miniature wheat stalks). Dried foliage can be purchased in crafts and floral supply stores.

• Use the twists that come with trash bags to make *Sansevieria* (snake plants). Separate the wire ties at the top, but leave them joined at the bottom. Trim the tops into spear shapes, and paint with green, white, and yellow (copy the real thing—there are different patterns: chevrons and stripes). Coil the stems, bend the leaves a bit, and plant in soil made of coffee grounds or sand. (For an example of a *Sansevieria* see *Rousseau*, page 72.)

• For landscaping rocks, use the real thing, or make them out of papier-mâché.

• Plastic or vinyl window coverings, sold in rolls in home decorating and hardware stores, have rippled surfaces that resemble *frozen ponds.* Cut the plastic to shape, and adhere to a sheet of Plexi in opaque white, smoke, blue transparent, or clear.

• To make a *bonsai tree,* use a bit of dried grape stem covered with lichen and hobby grass. The container can be a button, a computer key, or any other tiny receptacle, painted with matte hobby paint to look like stone or other organic material.

• To make a *garden path,* use sandpaper (which can be lightly sprayed with paint), aquarium gravel, bird-seed, cat litter, railroad foam, or the like. If using coffee grounds or real soil, first paint a coat of white glue on the path, then sprinkle on the grounds or soil. When the glue dries, blow off any excess. Lighter-weight materials can stick with spray mount, and heavier materials, like litter or gravel, will stick with white glue. When using paint to represent a path, mix it with sand or talcum powder for added texture.

• To make *trees,* build armatures out of wire, and coat the trunks and branches with self-hardening clay, putty, plaster, spackling compound, or papier-mâché. When dry, paint with hobby paints mixed with fine sand for texture. If possible, insert the trees into a drilled hole in the base of your model.

DRAINAGE CULVERT, 1992. 12 X 14 X 6 inches. *A desolate, Central Park nocturne. The street lamp's glow is from a plastic pearl.*

SOURCES

MUSEUMS

The Art Institute of Chicago
111 South Michigan Avenue
Chicago, Illinois 60603
312-443-3600
Look for: The Thorne Rooms.

Cullen Gardens and Miniature Village
300 Taunton Road, Whitby
Ontario, Canada L1N 5RS
Email: Cgardens@durham.net

The Doll House Museum
Station Road, Petworth
West Sussex, England
011-44-1798-344044

France Miniature
25 Route du Mesnil
F-78990
Elancourt, France
011-33-1-30-62-40-78

Kansas City Toy & Miniature
Museum
5235 Oak Street
Kansas City, Missouri 64112
816-333-2055

Lower East Side Tenement Museum
90 Orchard Street
New York, New York 10002
212-431-0233
Look for: one-inch scale replica of an
entire tenement building from the past.

Metropolitan Museum of Art
Fifth Avenue at 82nd Street
New York, New York 10028
212-879-5500
Look for: Crib of the Infant Jesus and
Egyptian house.

Miniature World
649 Humboldt Street
Victoria, British Columbia
Canada V8W 1A7
250-385-9731
www.miniatureworld.com

Musée de la miniature
19, rue Pierre Julien (face a la Poste),
26200 Montélimar
Drome, France
011-04-75-53-79-24
www.guideweb.com/musee/miniature

Museum of the City of New York
Fifth Avenue at 103rd Street
New York, New York 10029
212-534-1672
Look for: Dollhouse collection, including Florine Stettheimer dollhouse and
theater maquettes.

Museum of Miniature Houses and
Other Collections, Inc.
111 East Main Street
Carmel, Indiana 46032
317-575-9466
www.museumofminiatures.org

Museum of Miniatures
57 Fourth Avenue West
Cardston, Alberta TOK OKO
403-653-1142

Museum of Science & Industry
Home of the Colleen Moore Fairy
Castle
57th Street & Lake Shore Drive
Chicago, Illinois 60637
312-684-1414

Puppenhausmuseum Basel
(Doll's House Museum)
Steineck-Stiftung
Steinenvorstadt 1
CH-4051 Basel
011-41-61-225-95-95
www.puppenhausmuseum.ch

Queens Museum of Art
New York City Building
Flushing Meadows—Corona Park
Queens, New York 11368
718-592-9700
www.queensmuse.org
Look for: Replica of New York City in
its miniature entirety.

Strong Museum
One Manhattan Square
Rochester, New York 14607
716-263-2700
Look for: Dollhouse collection.

Tee Ridder Miniatures Museum at the
Nassau County Museum of Art
15 Museum Drive
Roslyn, New York 11576
516-484-9338
www.nassaumuseum.org

Washington Doll's House & Toy
Museum
5236 44th Street, NW
Washington, DC 20015
(202) 244-0024

Whitney Museum of American Art
945 Madison Avenue
New York, New York 10021
212-570-3600
Look for: Alexander Calder's miniature
circus; Charles Simmons' miniature
village.

SHOPS

MacKenzie-Childs
824 Madison Avenue
New York, New York 10021
212-570-6050; 888-665-1999
Look for: The Miniature Mansion,
with quarter-size replicas of the furnishings sold in this unusual shop and
restaurant.

Felissimo
10 West 56th Street
New York, New York 10019
212-247-5656

WEB SITES

www.avemariagrotto.com
*"Jerusalem in Miniature," which presents
in miniature historic buildings and
shrines of the world. These were created as
the lifetime work of a Benedictine monk
of St. Bernard Abbey, in Alabama.*

www.dhminiatures.com
The website of Dollhouse Miniatures
*magazine, which covers the art and craft
of miniatures and lists helpful and interesting internet sources.*

www.madurodam.nl
*A vast, miniature city in the Netherlands.
In a virtual tour of the model shop, you'll
see how exact replicas of real buildings are
created from blueprints. There are also
gardens with over 5,000 miniature trees.*

www.miniatures.about.com
*Provides international museum
information.*

SUPPLIES

Plastruct
www.plastruct.com
*A supplier of hobby and architectural
model components for, and books about,
making dioramas, doll houses, miniatures,
model railroading; and products for
scratch-building, special effects, etc. Their
products are found in hobby and model
train shops.*

Chrysnbon
www.deesdelights.com
*Realistic, detailed, inexpensive plastic
dollhouse furniture and accessories kits
(favorites among miniaturists for kit-
bashing). Products can be purchased or
ordered from dollhouse shops.*

Micro-Mark, "The Small Tool
Specialists"
800-225-1066
www.micromark.com
*Offers all kinds of helpful tools for
miniaturists.*

Right:
NIGHT PROWL, 1992. 15 x 24 x 18 inches.
*This piece began with a toy taxicab that I
found in the street. Around it I built the
vacant lot scene, mostly from a discarded air
conditioner. The security gate at the right is a
tin can flattened by a car.*

BIBLIOGRAPHY

AND SUGGESTED READING

CRAFTING

Anderson, Ray, *The Art of the Diorama*, Kalmbach Books, 1989

Barham, Andrea, *Easy to Make Dolls' House Accessories,* East Sussex: Guild of Master Craftsmen Publications, Ltd., 1995

Barnard, Lionel and Michael Hinchcliffe, *The Dolls' House Gardener,* David & Charles, Newton Abbot, Devon, 1999

Robinson, Peter, *Containers*, DK Publishing, Inc., New York, 1999

Wright, Michael, *Mixed Media: An Introduction,* Dorling Kindersley in association with the Royal Academy of Arts, London, 1995

ART HISTORY

Caws, Mary Ann (editor), *Joseph Cornell's Theater of the Mind,* Thames & Hudson, New York/London, 1993

McShine, Kynaston (editor), *Joseph Cornell,* The Museum of Modern Art, New York, 1990

O'Doherty, Brian, *American Masters: The Voice and the Myth, with photographs by Hans Namuth,* Random House, New York, 1973

Simic, Charles, *Dime-Store Alchemy: The Art of Joseph Cornell,* Ecco Press, New York, 1992

MINIATURE ART

Akre, Nancy (editor), *Miniatures*, Cooper-Hewitt Museum, New York, 1983

Benson, Arthur Christopher, *Everybody's Book of the Queen's Dolls' House,* Metheun & Co., Ltd., London, 1924

Buckland, Gail, *The White House in Miniature,* W.W. Norton & Co., New York, 1994

Culbert-Aguilar, Kathleen and Michael Anderson, *Miniature Rooms: The Thorne Rooms at the Art Institute of Chicago,* Abbeville Press, New York, 1983

Davis, Harry, *Tasha Tudor's Dollhouse: A Life in Miniatures,* Little, Brown, Boston, 1999

Gockerell, Nina, *Krippen Nativity Scenes and Creches,* Taschen, Koln, 1998

Goodfellow, Caroline G., *Dolls' Houses,* Her Majesty's Stationery Office, London, 1976

Jacobs, Flora Gill, *A History of Dolls' Houses,* Scribners, New York, 1953, 1965

Kamps, Toby, *Small World: Dioramas in Contemporary Art,* Museum of Contemporary Art San Diego, San Diego, 2000

Levinthal, David, *Modern Romance,* Essay by Eugenia Parry, St. Ann's Press, California, 2000

Moore, Gene and Jay Hyams, *My Time at Tiffany's,* St. Martin's Press, New York, 1990

Musgrave, Clifford, *Queen Mary's Dolls' House and dolls belonging to H.M. the Queen,* Pitkin Pictorials, London, 1967

Neff, Terry Ann R. and Barbara Karant, *Within the Fairy Castle: Colleen Moore's Doll House at the Museum of Science and Industry,* Little, Brown, Chicago, 1997

Noble, John, *A Fabulous Dollhouse of the Twenties: The Famous Stettheimer Dollhouse at the Museum of the City of New York*, Dover, New York, 1976

INTERIOR DESIGN

Hohauser, Sanford, *Architectural and Interior Models,* Van Nostrand Reinhold, New York, 1982

Miller, Judith, *More Period Details,* Clarkson Potter, New York, 1999

Salvo, Dana, *Home Altars of Mexico,* University of New Mexico Press, Albuquerque, 1997

INSPIRATIONAL

Bachelard, Gaston, *The Poetics of Space: The Classic Look at How We Experience Intimate Places,* Beacon Press, Boston, 1969

Frank, Ellen Eve, *Literary Architecture,* University of California Press, Berkeley, 1979

Pickover, Clifford, A. *Chaos in Wonderland,* St. Martin's Griffin, New York, 1994

Purkiss, Diane, *Troublesome Things: A History of Fairies and Fairy Stories,* Allen Lane, The Penguin Press, Middlesex, 2000

Swift, Jonathan, *Gulliver's Travels,* Schocken Books, New York, 1984

CONTRIBUTING ARTISTS

Rosemary Butler lives in Coral Gables, Florida. Her fascination with miniatures derives from a background in stage design.

Eric Edelman received an MA in Fine Arts from New York University, where his concentration on printmaking and letterpress influenced his use of the printed word in his art. He has shown his work at the National Arts Club and at the Kouros Gallery, New York.

Katharine Forsyth lives in New York City, where for many years she co-owned Dollhouse Antics, a miniatures shop on Madison Avenue.

Susan Leopold is a New York–based sculptor and installation artist. She exhibits her work internationally and nationally and is represented by the Jean Albano Gallery, Chicago. Leopold is the recipient of several fellowships, including the 1989–90 Indo-American and Fulbright fellowships. Her work has been reviewed in numerous publications, and is included in the collections of the Brooklyn Museum of Art, The Los Angeles County Museum, and many corporations.

David Levinthal, an artist in New York City, has received a National Endowment for the Arts Fellowship and a Guggenheim Fellowship. In 1997 the International Center of Photography, New York, presented the retrospective

"David Levinthal: Work from 1977 to 1996." *David Levinthal: Modern Romance,* a book about his work that includes an essay by Eugenia Parry, was published in 2000 by St. Ann's Press.

Victoria and Richard MacKenzie-Childs are the husband-and-wife founders of MacKenzie-Childs Ltd., which produces a line of fantastical, original home furnishings and accessories. Their headquarters are in Aurora, in upstate New York, and their glorious and fun retail store is at 824 Madison Avenue in New York.

John Mackiewicz is an artist from Jersey City, New Jersey. He was "discovered" by the O.K. Harris Gallery when his sister, acting as his agent, brought in slides of his miniature Jersey City and New York bars, diners, and hotel rooms.

Barbara Minch teaches drawing and illustration and directs a master art-critiquing and exhibiting group.

Charles Mingus III, artist, filmmaker, and playwright, lives in New York. He exhibits his work in the U.S. and abroad, and is represented by the Alan Stone Gallery. He has also shown paintings and watercolors at the Museum of Modern Art, New York.

Diane Price is the recipient of various awards and has work in many private and corporate collections. Price's boxes

have been exhibited in numerous galleries and art centers throughout the country. She resides in New Jersey.

Tim Prythero lives in Albuquerque, New Mexico, and has exhibited his art all over the country. Among the corporations and museums that own his work are the Albuquerque Museum and the Roswell Art Museum. Prythero is represented by the O.K. Harris Gallery, New York.

David Malcolm Rose is an artist and architectural model-maker. An architectural regard for the ruins of old roads and their defunct services inspired him to build exact replica of those poignant places.

Alan Wolfson has extensive experience doing theater scenic design and construction. He has also built miniatures for special effects in commercials and movies such as *Airplane* and *The Arrival.* While at Disney Imagineering he has created development models for Tokyo Disneyland and other Disney venues.

INDEX